IndiaCONDENSED

IndiaCONDENSED

5000 years of history and culture

Anjana Motihar Chandra

Marshall Cavendish Editions

Series Editor: Melvin Neo
Project Editor (Revised edition): Shawn Wee
Cover Concept: Lynn Chin Nyuk Ling
Designer: Bernard Go Kwang Meng

Published by Marshall Cavendish Editions
An imprint of Marshall Cavendish International
1 New Industrial Road, Singapore 536196

Other Marshall Cavendish Offices:
Marshall Cavendish Ltd. 5th Floor, 32-38 Saffron Hill, London EC1N 8FH, UK • Marshall Cavendish Corporation. 99 White Plains Road, Tarrytown NY 10591-9001, USA • Marshall Cavendish International (Thailand) Co Ltd. 253 Asoke, 12th Flr, Sukhumvit 21 Road, Klongtoey Nua, Wattana, Bangkok 10110, Thailand • Marshall Cavendish (Malaysia) Sdn Bhd, Times Subang, Lot 46, Subang Hi-Tech Industrial Park, Batu Tiga, 40000 Shah Alam, Selangor Darul Ehsan, Malaysia

Marshall Cavendish is a trademark of Times Publishing Limited

National Library Board Singapore Cataloguing in Publication Data
Chandra, Anjana Motihar, 1959-
India condensed : 5000 years of history & culture / Anjana Motihar Chandra. – Singapore : Marshall Cavendish Editions, c2007.
p. cm.
Includes bibliographical references and index.
ISBN-13 : 978-981-261-620-3 (pbk.)
ISBN-10 : 981-261-620-9 (pbk.)

1. India – History. 2. India – Civilization. I. Title.

DS436
954—dc22   SLS2007029180

Printed in Singapore by KWF Printing Pte Ltd

PREFACE

This book is not an in-depth study of Indian history and culture. Instead it is an easy-to-read work which attempts to present India in a nutshell. While countless books have been written about the history and culture of this great country, most are comprehensive and extensive, providing detailed information as well as insightful interpretations of India's complicated past. For this reason, they may be perceived as cumbersome tomes by readers looking for basic facts and simple information. A book of this kind fulfils this need for brevity.

This book was written for the overseas Indian or non-Indian who is keen to familiarise himself with Indian history and culture. It presents all the major episodes of India's fascinating past, from the early days of the Indus Valley Civilisation to the traumatic partition of the Indian subcontinent and the post-independence years. The attempt, as far as possible, has been to present the basic information about each period of Indian history without delving into extensive interpretation and analysis.

Dates and certain details in this book, particularly those related to ancient Indian history, may vary from other sources. This is because of the absence of documented information about this period. However, the attempt has been to present reliable information about the history of India, as well as interesting details about its philosophy, religions, festivals, music, dance, films, literature, art and crafts.

CONTENTS

CONTENTS

CONTENTS

THE RESURGENCE OF INDIA 1525

India in The 21st Century *153*

CHRONOLOGY

HISTORICAL HIGHLIGHTS

2800 – 1900 BC	Indus Valley Civilisation
1700 – 500 BC	Vedic Civilisation
327 – 323 BC	Alexander The Great
321 – 185 BC	The Maurya Dynasty
185 – 73 BC	The Sunga Dynasty
73 – 28 BC	The Kanva Dynasty
28 BC – 250 AD	The Satavahana Dynasty
320 – 550 AD	The Gupta Dynasty

606 – 647 AD	Harshvardhana
1206 – 1526	The Delhi Sultanate
1526 – 1858	The Mughal Empire
1608 – 1858	The British East India Company
1858 – 1947	The British Raj
1947	Partition & Independence
1950	India Becomes A Republic

MAP OF INDIA

CHINA

•Jammu and Kashmir

PAKISTAN

•Himacha Pradesh

•Punjab

•Uttaranchal

•Haryana

•Rajasthan

•Uttar Pradesh

NEPAL

Sikkim•

BHUTAN

Arunachal Pradesh•

•Assam   Nagaland•

•Meghalaya

BANGLADESH

Manipur•

•Bihar

•Jharkhand

Tripura•   •Mizoram

•Gujarat

•Madhya Pradesh

•West Bengal

•Chhattisgarh

•Orissa

•Maharashtra

•Andhra Pradesh

Goa•

•Karnataka

Arabian Sea

•Kerala

•Tamil Nadu

Bay of Bengal

Adnaman Islands•

Nicobar Islands•

SRI LANKA

HISTORY

PREHISTORIC INDIA

Stone Age Settlements

The region of South Asia, comprising present-day India, Pakistan, Bangladesh and Afghanistan, was inhabited 500,000 years ago, according to archaeological evidence from Stone Age sites. These early Stone Age societies gave way to middle Stone Age Mesolithic communities. Bhimbetka, at the foothills of the Vindhya Mountains, near present-day Bhopal, Madhya Pradesh, was a middle Stone Age site. The paintings created on the walls of rock shelters about 9,000–10,000 years ago by the Bhimbetka people are the earliest art forms to be found in India. In 7000 BC, Neolithic communities emerged in Mehrgarh, in the area now occupied by Baluchistan, Pakistan. The Mesolithic hunter-gatherers evolved into farmers in Mehrgarh, the earliest settlement of its kind in South Asia.

Bhimbetka

Bhimbetka was a Mesolithic site which came into prominence because of its prehistoric rock paintings. The rock shelters at Bhimbetka, a UNESCO World Heritage Site, are made up of five clusters of natural rock and display graphic paintings of life during the middle Stone Age period. The paintings were discovered by accident in 1958 by archaeologist Dr V S Wakankar. He was travelling by train to Bhopal when he saw some unusual formations on the rock shelters. On closer inspection, they turned out to be prehistoric.

The paintings depict the life of the people living in the caves, as well as the animals and vegetation in the surrounding area. One rock, known as the 'Zoo Rock', has pictures of elephants, sambhar, bisons and deer, while another rock displays a peacock, snake and deer with the sun. Some of the rocks show hunting scenes with hunters carrying bows, arrows, swords and shields. In one of the caves, a drawing shows a bison chasing a hunter, while another rock displays a human figure with horned headgear and an animal mask. The paints used by the Mesolithic people at Bhimbetka were made of coloured earth, vegetable dyes, roots and animal fat. Brushes were fashioned from fibrous twigs.

Mehrgarh

Mehrgarh, situated in the Kachi plains to the west of the Indus River in what is now Baluchistan, Pakistan, was a Neolithic community in 7000 b.c. It is known as the earliest farming settlement in South Asia and the first to use pottery. The inhabitants of Mehrgarh lived in buildings made of mud-brick and cultivated barley and wheat as crops, using stone tools to harvest them. They also shaped ornaments with these tools. The communities, thought to be of indigenous origin, evolved over time—buildings grew larger and the range of handicrafts expanded to include basketry and cotton textiles. Seals made of terracotta and bone, and decorated with geometric designs, were also a popular item of manufacture. Tools and ornaments were interred with the dead; the Mehrgarh people buried their females with more goods than they did the males.

The Mehrgarh period is divided into Mehrgarh I (7000 BC–5500 BC), Mehrgarh II (5500 BC–4800 BC) and Mehrgarh III (4800 BC–3500 BC). Copper came into use at Mehrgarh by 5000 BC. The people used a variety of production processes, including stone and copper drills, and kilns and crucibles for melting copper.

By 3500 BC, Mehrgarh covered an area of 75 hectares and carried out trade with neighbouring communities in the Quetta Valley, evident from the discovery of lapis lazuli beads. Mehrgarh seems to have been abandoned between 2600 BC and 2000 BC, when the Indus Valley Civilisation started to develop.

ANCIENT INDIA

INDUS VALLEY CIVILISATION (2800 BC – 1900 BC)

The Indus Valley Civilisation was South Asia's first known urban settlement. It existed during the Bronze Age and is believed to have started around 2800 BC–2700 BC, reaching its zenith between 2600 BC and 1900 BC. The Indus Valley Civilisation, also known as the Harappan Civilisation after its first excavated city Harappa, developed in the vicinity of the Indus River and its tributaries, in present-day Pakistan and northwestern India. Harappa and the city of Mohenjo-Daro were the main centres of habitation. The two ancient cities are described as urban masterpieces because of their highly sophisticated layout and functional design, which were advanced for their time. In fact, the standard of civic life reached by the Indus people was believed to be on par with the Sumerians and higher than that of the ancient Babylonians and Egyptians.

Harappa and Mohenjo-Daro

Harappa and Mohenjo-Daro, set about 600 km apart from each other, were stable settlements with about 30,000 residents each. They were laid out in rectangular patterns and included palatial homes, hill citadels, granaries, wide roads and canals for irrigation. Public baths and a well-established drainage system with brick-lined sewers, probably the world's first urban sanitation system of its kind, completed the elaborate structure. The sophisticated planning of the Indus Valley cities indicates the existence of a civic administrative body.

The Indus Valley Civilisation

This ancient civilisation was discovered by chance when British engineers in the mid-1800s constructed a railway line linking Karachi to Punjab in present-day Pakistan and found kiln-baked bricks scattered at the site. Sir Alexander Cunningham, an amateur archaeologist and general in the British army, investigated the site and found some seals and other antiquities; he didn't, however, delve into the unusual find. It was only later, in 1921, that details of the Indus culture came to light with the excavation of Harappa in Punjab by Sir John Marshall, the director general of the Archaeological Survey of India. The city of Mohenjo-Daro in Sind, Pakistan, was discovered later and was almost fully excavated by 1931.

Way of Life

The economy of the Indus Valley Civilisation was based on agriculture and trade, probably with ancient Mesopotamia, as indicated by the presence of the distinctive Indus seals in Mesopotamia. The seals were carved with animal figures and a kind of pictographic script. The writing has not been successfully deciphered but is believed to be related to the Dravidian script. In fact the Indus people are likely to have been of Dravidian origin, with a culture akin to that of the Dravidians.

The discovery of several terracotta objects of art, including human figures, as well as weapons and tools made of bronze and copper, revealed the advanced cultural life of the Indus Valley Civilisation. The religious beliefs of the people bore similarities with Hinduism. The seals provide evidence of worship of the Mother Goddess, including the sacrifice of goats and other animals as offerings. Some of the seals also have representations of a god resembling the Hindu god Shiva—in one of the seals, he is depicted with three faces and a horned headdress.

The Indus Valley Dravidians are thought to have moved south with the coming of the Aryan invaders. The decline of the Indus Valley Civilisation after 1900 BC has also been attributed to frequent flooding and a decline in the agricultural land due to climatic changes. These factors may have caused economic hardships leading to a gradual decay in society.

BURIAL RITUALS

The Indus people had an elaborate burial ritual. They placed their dead in coffins and then buried them in brick chambers with their heads pointing towards the north. The bodies, adorned with ornaments, were buried along with a number of pots. In some cases, couples were buried together in the same grave.

ARYANS AND THE VEDIC AGE (1700 BC – 500 BC)

The Vedic Civilisation succeeded the Indus Valley Civilisation in ancient India, but there is conflicting historical evidence about its origins. One theory points to the migration of Indo-European tribes, possibly from Central Asia, Iran, Scandinavia or Russia, into northern India in 2000 BC. These nomadic tribals, known as Aryans, mingled with the Dravidians from the Indus Valley and eventually established what came to be known as the Vedic Civilisation. It was spread across the Sapta Sindhu (Seven Rivers) region, in the present-day Indian states of Haryana and Punjab.

The ancient Hindu scriptures, the *Vedas*, dated between 1500 BC and 800 BC, provide extensive details of the Vedic Civilisation: The *Rig-Veda*, the earliest document of Indian history, gives a comprehensive account of life in the early days of the Aryan society, while later works such as the *Sama-Veda*, *Yajur-Veda* and *Atharva-Veda* provide details about the subsequent years. The *Vedas* were composed in the Sanskrit language, and the Vedic Civilisation takes its name from these ancient scriptures. The great Indian epics, the *Ramayana* and the *Mahabharata*, are also believed to have originated during this period of Indian history. The Vedic age is divided into the Early Vedic Period (1700 BC–1000 BC) and the Later Vedic Period (1000 BC–500 BC).

Early Vedic Period

The Aryans were tall and fair in appearance. They organised their community into small tribal units called *jana*, with chiefs (*sabha*) and ruling councils (*samiti*). The *jana* was further divided into smaller segments called *vish* and *grama*. There were several *janas*, and they fought amongst each other for cattle and land. The *janas* developed into *janapadas*, small kingdoms with a supreme chief, the *raja* or king, who commanded the army. The king was assisted by the *senani* (army chief) and the *purohita* (chaplain), who took on the role of a medicine man, curing diseases with the use of incantation.

The Aryans had a primitive nomadic culture and did not have knowledge of sophisticated urban planning as seen in the Indus period. Rather, their houses were simple structures built of mud. However, like the Indus people, the Aryans were skilled in making bronze utensils and weapons. Their main occupation was cattle rearing and agriculture. Cattle were highly valued and used as a medium of exchange in the barter system. The people also bred sheep, goats and horses, using the latter for their war chariots. Spinning, weaving and carpentry were other common trades.

Aryans Introduce the Caste System

The Aryans had a patriarchal society, with the father regarded as the head of the family and the mother occupying an inferior position. Monogamy was widely practised, and sons were coveted because the family heritage passed from father to son. It was during the Vedic period that India's infamous caste system (*varna*) was born. Society was divided into separate classes based on occupation: the priests, known as Brahmins, were the dominant class and wielded the most power; the ruling and fighting classes were called Kshatriyas; traders and merchants were classified as Vaishyas and the labourers were known as the Shudras. Social distinctions became increasingly rigid and the classes developed into hereditary castes, with restrictions placed on intermarriage.

The religious consciousness of the Aryans was highly developed, although they did not pray at temples or worship images. Their rituals consisted of burning fires at home, singing hymns to the gods, making offerings such as rice and milk and sacrificing animals. The Aryan gods included Varuna (Thunder), Surya (Sun), Agni (Fire), Vayu (Wind) and Usha (Dawn).

BRAHMA AND THE CASTE SYSTEM

According to popular belief, the four *varnas* were created from different parts of Brahma, the creator. The Brahmins were created from his mouth, the Kshatriyas from his hands, the Vaishyas from his thighs and the Shudras from his feet.

Later Vedic Period

In the Later Vedic Civilisation, agriculture became the main economic activity of the people while cattle rearing declined. Popular crafts developed into vocations and goldsmiths, ironsmiths and carpenters came to the fore; iron, especially, became a commonly used metal during this period. Another change was the merging of the numerous small kingdoms or *janapadas* to create 16 large ones known as the *mahajanapadas* or great kingdoms. This period also saw progress in political and economic organisation, with a tight-knit monarchy replacing the earlier tribal rule. Power moved from the rural to the urban centres where noblemen usurped positions of authority. Strides were made in religious thought too, with ideas from a new Hindu culture taking root. The Aryans used the Vedic Sanskrit language up to the 6th century BC, when their culture gradually began to shift to Brahmanism, an early form of Hinduism. This marked the end of the Vedic Civilisation.

LAWS OF MANU

The Brahmins, the most learned sect, laid down rules and regulations, customs, laws and rites for the rest of society in manuals called the *Dharma-shastras*. Of these the most ancient and most famous is the *Manava Dharma-shastra* (Laws of Manu), belonging to the ancient Manava Vedic school. The Laws of Manu comprises of 2,684 verses and deals with the norms of domestic, social and religious life in India.

The Mahajanapadas and the Kingdom of Magadha

Magadha was among the most powerful of the 16 Aryan kingdoms known as the *mahajanapadas*. It was also in Magadha where the religions of Buddhism and Jainism flourished in ancient times, posing a threat to the existing Brahmanism. Magadha was situated in north India, in modern-day Bihar and Jharkhand. Its capital was originally Rajagriha (now Rajgir) and later shifted to Pataliputra (now Patna). The kingdom gained prominence under the rule of Bimbisara (543 BC–491 BC), who was a contemporary and staunch supporter of the Buddha, the founder of Buddhism. Rajgir is considered a sacred site in Buddhism as the Buddha spent many years preaching there, delivering his sermons in Magadhi, the language of Magadha and a dialect of Sanskrit. In fact, the city was the venue of the first Buddhist council held in 486 BC, after the Buddha's passing. The third Buddhist council was held at Pataliputra under the auspices of Emperor Ashoka of the Maurya dynasty. Besides the political and religious developments, Magadha and other kingdoms in northern India also witnessed a growth in agriculture between the 6th and 5th centuries BC.

The Mahajanapadas

There was also considerable progress in commerce during this period.

It was under King Bimbisara (543 BC–491 BC), who belonged to the Shishunaga dynasty, and later his son Ajatashatru, that Magadha achieved greatness. Bimbisara extended the empire by annexing the kingdom of Anga, now West Bengal, in the east. Ajatashatru, who was responsible for his father's death, continued the expansion and built a fortress at Pataliputra during his war with the Licchavi republic. The expansionist Shishunaga dynasty was overthrown by the Nandas in 343 BC. The Nanda dynasty, founded by Mahapadma, ruled Magadha until 321 BC. when it fell to Chandragupta who made it the centre of his Maurya Empire. Later, in the 4th century AD, Magadha rose to prominence once again during the Gupta period.

HORSE SACRIFICE

A popular royal ritual was the horse sacrifice or Ashwamedha Yagna. In this ritual, the king's horse, accompanied by warriors, was set free and allowed to go where it pleased for a full year. The territories covered by the horse during this period then came under the control of the king, with the warriors stepping in to enforce the king's claim of sovereignty in the case of opposition from the local inhabitants. The horse was slaughtered at the end of the ritual.

ALEXANDER THE GREAT (r. 327 BC – 323 BC)

Alexander the Great, acknowledged as one of the greatest military strategists of his time, was the first of the Greek conquerors to invade India. Alexander III, King of Macedonia, arrived in Punjab in 327 BC, after conquering the vast Persian Empire. Following the takeover of the cities of Taxila and Aornos in Punjab, in present-day Pakistan, he fought against the powerful Indian monarch Porus in the vicinity of the Hydaspes River (present-day Jhelum River) in the epic Battle of Hydaspes (326 BC). The Indians fought with elephants, a new phenomenon for the Greeks.

After his victory, Alexander struck an alliance with Porus and allowed him to continue to rule the kingdom. Alexander and his men then pressed on, to conquer the region along the Indus River, heading towards the Ganges River and the powerful kingdom of Magadha. On the way, the battle-weary soldiers mutinied and Alexander was forced to change direction. He went south down the Indus River and attacked villages on the way. Alexander and his men reached the mouth of the Indus in July 325 BC, after which they turned westward to return home. While in India, Alexander set up numerous Greek settlements which facilitated trade and communication with other parts of his empire.

Alexander, who believed in a fusion of different races, was keen to make Asia and Europe a single country with Babylon as the capital. He encouraged intermarriage as part of his universal policy and married a Persian princess himself. He promoted the dissemination of Greek customs in India and the rest of his empire in Asia.

Alexander's ambitious plans were thwarted when he suddenly fell ill at Babylon and died in June 323 BC at the age of 33. In the absence of a successor, his generals became governors of different regions and fought amongst themselves for control of the empire. By 311 BC, Alexander the Great's empire had split into independent states and monarchies. In India, little trace of his empire was left after his death, but the memory of Secunder, as he was called in India, lived on for years to come.

BUCEPHALUS—ALEXANDER'S FAVOURITE STEED

Legends abound about Alexander and his favourite steed Bucephalus. He is said to have fought many battles to victory and committed daring deeds while riding the horse. Alexander was heartbroken when Bucephalus died during the Battle of Hydaspes. He founded the city of Bucephala in the region in the horse's memory.

THE MAURYA DYNASTY (321 BC – 185 BC)

CHANDRAGUPTA MAURYA:
THE MONARCH WHO UNIFIED INDIA (r. 321 BC – 297 BC)

The Maurya Empire was ancient India's largest and most powerful sovereign state, encompassing most of the subcontinent except for a small area in the south. Founded by Chandragupta Maurya, who overthrew Danananda, the last king of the Nanda dynasty of Magadha to conquer the kingdom in 321 BC, it had an efficient and highly organised bureaucratic structure complete with a civil service. Chandragupta was aided in his conquest by his prime minister, Kautilya, also known as Chanakya, a scheming adviser who has been likened to Machiavelli. Kautilya left behind *Arthasastra*, an acclaimed treatise on statecraft, describing laws and administrative procedures and dispensing political advice.

After taking over Magadha, Chandragupta went on to conquer Taxila in neighbouring Punjab. Gradually, he and his son Bindusura extended the Maurya Empire north to the Himalayas, east to Persia and far south, leaving out only a tribal stretch near Kalinga.

It was in c.305 BC that Chandragupta won over parts of Afghanistan from Alexander the Great's satrap Seleucus and liberated the trans-Indus region from Greek occupation. Chandragupta concluded a peace treaty with Seleucus and gave the Greek 500 war elephants in exchange for the occupied territory.

Through his conquests, Chandragupta was able to unify India's disparate kingdoms under a strong centralised government for the first time. Pataliputra where the administration was located, became the capital of the empire. The basic unit of Chandragupta's administration was the village, which had a headman and a village council. Groups of villages made up districts, which in turn grouped together into provinces administered by governors. Due to its unified structure, the empire developed a strong economy, with internal and external trade thriving and agriculture flourishing. Punch-marked silver coins with symbols from nature were in use in the Maurya Empire. Chandragupta's religious tolerance gave a fillip to social reform. A paranoid ruler who constantly feared for his life, Chandragupta eventually abdicated to become a Jain monk. He was succeeded by his son Bindusura who consolidated the power and influence of the empire before passing on the mantle to his own son Ashokavardhan, known as Ashoka the Great for the respect he commanded in the kingdom.

KAUTILYA'S STORY HELPS WIN MAGADHA

According to legend, Chandragupta was able to overthrow the Nanda dynasty in Magadha after drawing inspiration from a story related by Kautilya about a little boy and a plate of food. Kautilya described how the boy stuck his hand into the middle of his favourite dish and burned his fingers. Drawing an analogy between the dish and a kingdom, he said that just as the centre was the hottest part of the dish, similarly, the centre of a kingdom was the most challenging section to take over. To be victorious, Kautilya advised Chandragupta to strike at the frontiers first, then advance to the middle. This strategy worked and Chandragupta achieved victory in Magadha.

ASHOKA THE GREAT (r. 273 BC – 232 BC)

Ashoka's Empire

Chandragupta's grandson, Ashoka, is regarded as India's greatest emperor. He was the last major monarch of the Maurya dynasty and is best known for his espousal of Buddhism and for promoting it to the status of a world religion. He also made a significant contribution to the development of Indian culture.

Ashoka was a fearless commander and a shrewd statesman who came to power in 273 BC. He continued the conquests begun by his grandfather, extending the Maurya Empire to include present-day Bangladesh, as well as Afghanistan. However, his bloody takeover of the state of Kalinga (now Orissa) in c.265 BC, proved to be a turning point in his life. Ashoka was hit by remorse at the bloodshed caused by his military and decided to renounce aggression forever. Ashoka converted to Buddhism and became one of its staunchest supporters.

Rise of Buddhism under Ashoka's Patronage

Ashoka helped spread Buddhism throughout his empire and beyond, to China, Japan and the Far East. He inscribed Buddhist teachings on stones and pillars as part of his famous Ashoka Edicts. The most renowned of Ashoka's pillars was at Sarnath, in present-day Uttar Pradesh. Known as the Ashoka Pillar, it is a column built with a sculpture of four lions on its head. The sculpture is called the Lion Capital and was adopted as the national emblem of India under British colonial rule. The sculpture was eventually removed from the Ashoka Pillar and placed in the Sarnath Museum.

Ashoka also propagated Buddhism by building monasteries and dome-shaped monuments known as stupas. The most notable of these was at Sanchi, in present-day Madhya Pradesh, built to house relics of the Buddha. The third Buddhist council at Pataliputra was held in 250 BC under Ashoka's sponsorship. After the council, Ashoka sent monks, as well as his twin children Mahindra and Sanghamitra, to foreign lands to spread the message of Buddhism.

On the political front, Ashoka softened the laws introduced by his grandfather and father, and preached justice and non-violence (*ahimsa*). He also banned hunting and unnecessary animal slaughter, and abolished forced labour. On the international front, Ashoka improved relations with countries in Asia and Europe. His reign was marked by peace and stability; it was a time when art and other creative pursuits flourished and the empire prospered.

The Maurya Empire, which reached its pinnacle under Ashoka's benign leadership, declined after his death in 232 BC.

ASHOKA'S EDICTS

> Ashoka's teachings, wisdom and remarkable achievements have lived on through the thousands of rocks and pillars he inscribed with his famous edicts. The inscriptions are in the Brahmi script and have been found scattered across India, Nepal, Pakistan and Afghanistan. In his edicts, Ashoka wrote about the reforms he introduced to create a just and humane society, as well as the religious and moral values and principles that were dear to his heart.

POST-ASHOKA PERIOD

The Sunga Dynasty (185 BC – 73 BC)

The last Maurya ruler, Brhadratha, was assassinated at a military parade in 185 BC by Pusyamitra Sunga, the commander-in-chief of the Mauryan armed forces. Pusyamitra Sunga, who was a follower of Brahmanism, went on to establish the Sunga dynasty which ruled for about 100 years. Under his rule, Buddhism went through a decline after reaching its heyday under Emperor Ashoka and his successors. Pusyamitra ordered the persecution of followers of Buddhism and the destruction of stupas and monasteries. However, despite the government clampdown, the religion retained its following and continued to be practised in some areas. Pusyamitra's empire, a loose federal structure, stretched from Pataliputra, the capital, to Ayodhya, Vidisa, Jalandhara and Sakala. While he continued the Mauryan practice of administering the provinces through princes, control was decentralised and nuclear kingdoms were allowed to exist within the empire.

The Kanva Dynasty (73 BC – 28 BC)

Pusyamitra's reign was marked by numerous military campaigns against the Yavanas, or the Indo-Greeks, who attempted to invade the region from Bactria, present-day northern Afghanistan. Pusyamitra ruled for 36 years, after which his successors continued the dynasty until about 73 BC. Devabhuti, the last Sunga leader, was overthrown by one of his own ministers, Vasudeva Kanva, who established the Kanva dynasty. The Kanva reign in Magadha lasted until 28 BC when the region was taken over by the Satavahanas, also known as the Andhras.

The Satavahana Dynasty (28 BC – 250 AD)

Members of the Satavahana dynasty belonged to the Andhra tribe. They were part of the Maurya Empire and founded their own kingdom in the north-western part of the Deccan plateau, during the decline of the Maurya dynasty. Gradually the Satavahana rulers, such as Satakarni I, extended their territory across the northern Deccan to central India.

In the year 100, they lost power to invading foreign tribes, the Sakas, and were eventually left with the present-day Andhra region of southern India. They regained the lost land in the year 200. By 250, the Satavahana kingdom had disintegrated, breaking up into small pockets ruled by different branches of the family. Satavahana rule was marked by peace, prosperity and religious tolerance, with both Brahmanism and Buddhism being practised by the people.

GREEK AND CENTRAL ASIAN INVADERS

Indo-Greek Kingdom (175 BC – 10 BC)

Beginning around 180 BC, the northern part of the Indian subcontinent was invaded by a series of foreign armies from Central Asia. The Indo-Greeks were the first to come, led by Greco-Bactrian leader Demetrius, who established the Indo-Greek Kingdom in the region in 175 BC. Demetrius created a state which seceded from the powerful Greco-Bactrian Kingdom in Bactria (today's northern Afghanistan). One of his successors was Menander who, along with Demetrius, is credited with extending the power and influence of the Indo-Greek Kingdom. Taxila in Punjab was one of the many capitals of the kingdom. It was ruled by a succession of over 30 Hellenistic kings during almost two centuries of Indo-Greek rule.

Greek, Buddhist and Hindu art, culture, languages and symbols came together in an interesting fusion during this period, evident from excavated Indo-Greek coins and other archaeological remains. Of particular significance is Greco-Buddhist art which combines the realism of Hellenistic creativity with symbols of Buddhism. The Indo-Greeks vanished around 10 BC when the region was invaded by Central Asian tribes such as the Scythians, followed by the Yuezhis from China and the Parthians, who established their own kingdoms in the region.

Indo-Scythian, Kushan and Indo-Parthian Kingdoms

The Scythians, also known as Sakas, came to India from Central Asia in 10 BC in search of new territory after invading Bactria. Maues, or Moga, was one of the early Scythian leaders in India and ruled over Gandhara, in present-day northern Pakistan. He gradually extended his empire to the north-west, until the arrival of the Yuezhis from China, who conquered the area and set up the Kushan Empire. In the 1st century, invading Parthian leader Gondophares established the Indo-Parthian kingdom, which extended from northern India to Afghanistan and Pakistan. However, Parthian rule only lasted until the year 75 AD when the region was annexed by the Kushans again.

King Kanishka (r. 78–111)

The most powerful leader of the Kushans was Kanishka, King of Gandhara. Like Mauryan Emperor Ashoka, Kanishka was known for his patronage of Buddhism. During his reign, he built Buddhist stupas, the most notable being the Kanishka stupa at Peshawar, and developed Buddhist art by helping to establish the Gandhara School of Art. Coins made during Kanishka's rule were embellished with Buddhist, Hindu, Greek and Persian images, evidence of his religious tolerance. Kanishka is said to have convened the fourth Buddhist council in c.100.

Kanishka was an ambitious monarch who was keen to control the entire territory of Central Asia. To this end, he made conquests in the Indian subcontinent and beyond. At its height, his empire stretched from the Pamir mountain range in Central Asia to Bengal in the Indian subcontinent, with the capital at Peshawar. Kanishka's successors failed to maintain his power or influence; by the middle of the 3rd century, the Kushans were left with only Gandhara and Kashmir.

GANDHARA SCHOOL OF ART

The Gandhara art style featured scenes from Buddhist texts and images of the Buddha, some of which were based on the Greek god Apollo. Images from this school showed the Buddha as a short, stocky form, either seated or standing. The eyes in most of the statues were open with a circle between the brows, and the hands were depicted resting in the lap in a gesture of repose, or with the right hand touching the earth.

THE GUPTA EMPIRE 320–550

Chandragupta I (r. 320–335)

The Gupta Empire came into existence in 320 AD at a time when the Indian subcontinent, unified under the erstwhile Maurya dynasty, had become fragmented and divided into small kingdoms and republics. Under Gupta rule, India's past glory was revived in an atmosphere of peace and stability. In fact, the Gupta dynasty's reign is known as the Golden Age in Indian history for the rapid strides made in education, science, architecture, sculpture, painting and Sanskrit literature, under the patronage of the monarchs. As India's culture came into its own during this period, Hinduism was established as the major religion, trade flourished and textiles became a booming industry with silk, cotton, muslin and linen exported to foreign lands.

Chandragupta I is credited with having founded the Gupta dynasty and the Gupta Empire, although the first known member of the Gupta clan was Sri Gupta, the grandfather of Chandragupta I. Chandragupta I was a local chief in the kingdom of Magadha whose influence grew after a marital alliance with Princess Kumaradevi of the influential Lichchavi clan from present-day Nepal. He gained control of the strategic Ganges Valley and proclaimed himself Maharajadhiraya, 'King of Kings'. Like his namesake Chandragupta Maurya, he set up his capital at Pataliputra and consolidated his empire across the Ganges Valley and Magadha.

Samudragupta (r. 335–380)

Chandragupta I's warrior son, Samudragupta, who succeeded him, was a statesman and a brilliant strategist. He waged countless military campaigns during his rule, which lasted for nearly half a century. He extended the Gupta Empire to Punjab in the north, Assam in the east and to the Deccan Plateau in the south. Samudragupta is hailed as one of India's greatest military geniuses and is referred to as the Napoleon of India.

Besides his military prowess, Samudragupta was known for his remarkable skill in poetry and music. He composed many works of poetry during his reign, and was lauded for his creativity in literature and classical music. Coins that were minted during Samudragupta's rule show him playing on the *veena*, an Indian string instrument. He was also known to be tolerant towards other faiths even though he himself followed the Hindu religion and was a devotee of Vishnu. Samudragupta was succeeded by his son, Ramagupta, who was a weak ruler and had a brief reign. Ramagupta was assassinated by his brother, Chandragupta II, also called Vikramaditya, who was considered the greatest of the Gupta rulers.

CHANDRAGUPTA II (r. 380–415)

The Gupta Empire reached its zenith under Chandragupta II who continued the expansionist policies of his father and grandfather. One of his greatest achievements was the defeat of the independent Shaka principalities in the Gujarat region of western India. He also had patronage over the Vataka Empire in the Maharashtra and Madhya Pradesh region following the marriage of his daughter, Prabhavatigupta, with Vataka ruler Rudrasena II. With these developments, Chandragupta II was able to take the Gupta Empire to its

Map of Gupta Empire at end of 4th Century

height, strategically placed as it was to control the prosperous trade routes to the West. He led a strong government in an atmosphere of peace, prosperity and political and cultural unity. Ujjain, in Madhya Pradesh, was the second capital of his empire.

We have a detailed account of the opulence of Chandragupta II's reign through the writings of Chinese Buddhist monk Fa Hsien who travelled to India in 399 in search of Buddhist texts. He also described the just nature of the Gupta administration and the vast spread of the empire. Gold coins also provide evidence of the grandeur of Chandragupta II's court. These coins, bearing images of the Gupta rulers, were carried outside India to other parts of Asia by traders.

Chandragupta II was succeeded by his son, Kumaragupta, in 415. Kumaragupta ruled for about 40 years and was succeeded by Skandagupta, considered the last of the great Gupta rulers. The remaining Gupta rulers included Narasimhagupta, Kumaragupta II, Buddhagupta and Vishnugupta.

The Golden Age of Indian History

The Gupta kings presided over the Golden Age in Indian history. It was under their benign leadership that India's arts and sciences flourished as never before. In art and architecture, the murals in the caves at Ajanta, Maharashtra, stand out for their skillful craftsmanship. Most of the murals in the 30 caves are believed to have been created between 460 and 480. They depict the life of the Buddha and represent other scenes and symbols from Buddhism. The famous Iron Pillar in Delhi is a legacy from the era of Chandragupta II.

IRON PILLAR OF DELHI

The Iron Pillar in the Indian capital Delhi is a metallurgical curiosity because it has withstood corrosion since it was built during the reign of Chandragupta II, due, apparently, to its high phosphorus content. The pillar is almost seven metres high with an idol of the mythical bird Garuda on top. It was originally located at a place called Vishnupadagiri near present-day Bhopal, Madhya Pradesh.

The Gupta rulers built universities, monasteries and free hospitals to improve the quality of life of their people and provide them with new avenues of learning. The Buddhist monastery of Nalanda, near Patna, Bihar, had pride of place among Indian universities of that period. Trade helped to export the culture of the Gupta Empire to other countries such as Burma, Cambodia and Sri Lanka, where it left a deep impact.

The Gupta rulers were great patrons of literature and poetry, particularly in the Sanskrit language, which reached spectacular heights under their reign. Buddhist and Jain literature, produced earlier in Prakrit, dialects of Sanskrit, began to appear in classical Sanskrit. Notable writers and poets from this period include Kalidasa, a master of his craft, Dandi, Visakhadatta, Shudraka and Bharavi. Noteworthy works from the Gupta period include Kalidasa's masterpiece *Abhijnana Shakuntala*; *Kamasutra* on the art of love by Vatsyayana; and Panchatantra, a renowned collection of fables which is said to have inspired the *Fables of Aesop* and *A Thousand and One Nights*. The Hindu epic, the *Mahabharata*, was rewritten during this period. Most of the literary works sang the praises of Hindu gods, as the tenets of Hinduism crystallised and the religion grew in significance under royal patronage. Under the new style of worship, temples were built and dedicated to a particular god.

Significant progress was also made in mathematics with the development of the Indian numerical and decimal system. Books on medicine, veterinary science, mathematics, astronomy and astrophysics were penned. Astronomy was a growing discipline, with the brilliant astronomers, Aryabhata and Varahamihira, belonging to this age. It was at this time that Aryabhata made his discoveries of pi as 3.1416 and the length of the solar year as 365.358 days.

KALIDASA

Kalidasa, considered as the greatest Indian poet and playwright, was believed to be one of the nine gems, or most learned men, of Chandragupta II's court. He excelled in lyric poetry and drama and is best known for his second play in Sanskrit, *Abhijnana Shakuntala*, an all-time classic of world literature which has been translated in many Indian and foreign languages. Legend goes that Kalidasa was a devotee of the Hindu goddess Kali, hence his name meaning 'Kali's slave'. Kali rewarded him with an extraordinary gift of wit, which endeared him to King Chandragupta II. Kalidasa wrote three plays, *Malavikagnimitra*, *Abhijnana Shakuntala* and *Vikramorvashe*; the lyric *Meghadutta*; and two epic poems *Raghuvamsha* and *Kumarasambhava*. *Abhijnana Shakuntala* is a poignant tale of love and separation, revolving around Shakuntala, a forest nymph who bewitches King Dushyanta while he is out hunting. Kalidasa is believed to have been inspired by the character of Shakuntala in the Hindu epic, the *Mahabharata*.

Decline of the Gupta Empire and the Hun Invasion

The Gupta Empire, under the rule of Skandagupta, fell prey to the Huns or Hunas, tribals who originated from the north of China. The Huns had settled in northern and central India by 454 and posed a constant threat to the Gupta Empire. Skandagupta spent the last 12 years of his reign warding off attacks from the tribe, which considerably weakened the empire. In 510, the Huns, led by Mihirakula, conquered Punjab, Gujarat and Malwa, leaving the Guptas to rule over Bengal. The last of the Gupta kings, Vishnugupta, who reigned over a vastly diminished kingdom, died in 550. With the demise of the Gupta Empire, northern India was split into independent kingdoms once again, signifying an end to the political unity the region had enjoyed.

POST-GUPTA PERIOD

Harshvardhana: A Secular Scholar (r. 606–647)

It was decades later, in 606, that the fragmented states of northern India came together again under the strong leadership of Harshvardhana, a scion of the Vardhana dynasty of the kingdom of Thaneswar. By this time, 'India', as a single entity, was perceived to stretch from the Himalayas to the southern tip at Kanyakumari.

Harshvardhana was only 16 when he ascended the throne upon the death of his father and brother. but the young monarch proved to be a unifying force and succeeded in building an empire stretching from Gujarat in the west to Bengal in the east and Kashmir in the north.

Chinese Buddhist monk Hsuan Tsang, who visited India in 630 during Harshvardhana's reign, is full of praise for the monarch, whom he describes as generous, talented and energetic. Harshvardhana was an able leader and administrator who kept in touch with his people by travelling extensively in his kingdom. He often visited his subjects in disguise so he could get a first hand view of their problems. He had a tolerant, secular approach to religion and was himself a follower of both Hinduism and Buddhism. In 644, he held a Buddhist Council at Kanauj, in Uttar Pradesh state during Hsuan Tsang's visit. Like the Gupta rulers before him, Harshvardhana was a scholar who enjoyed literature and promoted it during his reign. He himself wrote several plays, with religion or comedy as the theme. Harshvardhana died in 647 without an heir. His death brought an end to the rule of the Vardhana dynasty in north India.

RISE OF THE RAJPUTS

The Rajputs are Hindu warriors who came into prominence in the 7th century in north-western and central India. Historians are divided as to their origins, with some claiming they are of Aryan lineage, and others describing them as descendants of the invading Huns and Central Asian Shaka tribes. According to one legend, the Rajputs emerged from a ritual fire to defend the Brahmin caste.

The Rajput Kingdoms

The Rajputs are divided into four clans: Chauhan, Solanki, Parmaar and Pratihara. Each clan established a small independent kingdom in north-western and central India and they fought amongst themselves for greater power and influence. Almost all the kingdoms in this region were ruled by

Rajputs, and their governments were feudal in nature. Each kingdom was split into provinces known as *jagirs* which were controlled by a *jagirdar* who was from the same clan as the king. One prominent leader of the Rajput Chauhan dynasty was Prithviraj Chauhan, who was extolled for his fearlessness and heroic deeds.

THE HEROIC DEEDS OF PRITHVIRAJ CHAUHAN

> Prithviraj Chauhan became a romantic hero for the Rajputs when he fell in love with the daughter of his enemy, the king of the kingdom of Kanauj, and eloped with her. According to legend, the king wished to get his daughter married and held a gathering of prospective suitors for her to choose from. He purposely left Prithviraj out, using instead a statue to represent him. When the girl was asked to make her choice among the assembled men, she placed a garland around the statue. Prithviraj, hiding nearby, then rode in to the hall and gallantly carried her off to be his bride.

The Dark Age of India

The Rajputs are largely known for their valour and passion for battle, but the arts and architecture also blossomed under their regime. The Sun Temple at Konarak in Orissa, which is shaped like a stone chariot, exemplifies the creativity of this period. However, despite the heroism of the Rajputs and their patronage of the arts, this period is referred to as the Dark Age of India. This is because under the Rajputs, social evils such as the caste system were rigidly enforced. The severity of the caste system peaked during this period when many new castes were added to the original four. Child marriage, polygamy, the persecution of Buddhists and the practice of *sati*—widow immolation on her husband's pyre—were other social evils that were rampant under the Rajputs. Female infanticide was also common because the Rajputs perceived the birth of a daughter as ignominious. One of the most celebrated women in Rajput history is Mira Bai, who was married at the age of 13 and left her home to devote her life to the Hindu god Krishna after the early death of her husband.

The power and influence of the Rajputs diminished temporarily during the Mughal invasion in the 17th century. Under the British, many of the

Rajput princes maintained independent states in the region of Rajputana, now Rajasthan.

THE SOUTHERN KINGDOMS

The southern part of the Indian subcontinent was ruled by royal dynasties in relative peace and stability, even as north India was being conquered by foreign invaders. This region, with the Deccan Plateau at its core, stretches from the Vindhya range of mountains to Kanyakumari at the tip of India, and from the Arabian Sea in the west to the Bay of Bengal in the east. Trade with the Roman Empire and Arab merchants was a major source of revenue for the southern kingdoms, whose strategic location put them in greater contact with foreign lands.

While the Satavahanas (also known as Andhras) dominated the Deccan Plateau, further south in Tamil Nadu, power was shared by the three warring kingdoms of Pandyas, Cheras and Cholas, after the decline of the Pallava dynasty. The Pandyas had control of Madurai, the Cheras controlled the south-western coast and the Cholas dominated Thanjavur. Tamil was the main language of these Dravidian rulers, and Tamil literature and poetry blossomed under their patronage.

The Tamil kingdoms are known for their magnificent temples with idols of the gods cast in gold and silver, and embedded with jewels, as well as their palace culture, complete with musicians and dancers, known as *devadasis*, to invoke the gods. Hinduism was widespread in the south, but there were pockets of Christianity too, beginning in the 1st century when Jesus' disciple St Thomas landed on the Malabar Coast and brought the message of Christianity to India.

The Pallava Dynasty (4th–9th Centuries)

The Pallavas established their capital at Kanchipuram by 325 and ruled the south for at least 500 years. Kanchipuram was called the Golden City for its temples, numbering over 100. It was also an important centre of Hindu and Buddhist culture. The Pallavas are best known for their patronage of Dravidian architecture, a splendid example being the Seven Pagodas of Mahabalipuram, the main seaport of their empire.

It was during this period that religious fervour reached its peak, and Hinduism saw a shift from the worship of Vedic gods to devotion to the trinity of Brahma, Vishnu and Shiva. At around this time, renowned Kerala philosopher Adi Shankaracharya founded the Vedanta School of thought that encouraged debate on the *Vedas* and propagated the philosophy of non-duality, or attaining the Supreme Consciousness (*brahman*) by detaching oneself from the material plane (*maya* or illusion). The Pallava kingdom was involved in constant battle with the Chalukyas of Badami, but it was at the hands of the Chola kings that it suffered defeat in the 9th century.

The Chola Dynasty (9th–13th Centuries)

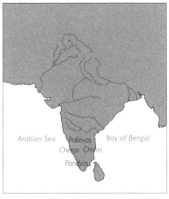

The Southern Kingdoms

The Chola dynasty gained prominence at the end of the 9th century after it overthrew the Pallava rulers. The Cholas reached the pinnacle of their power under Raja Raja Chola I (985–1014) and Rajendra I (1014–1042). Raja Raja I brought stability to the kingdom and extended its power with the conquest of neighbouring Kerala and northern Sri Lanka. His successor, Rajendra, took over the entire island of Sri Lanka and occupied areas in Burma, Malaya and Sumatra. The Chola years were marked by the blossoming of literature and the arts, particularly temple architecture. Raja Raja I built enormous temple complexes at Thanjavur, the capital of the kingdom, with each temple associated with a fascinating legend. The Brihadeeswara temple, dedicated to the Hindu god Shiva, is unmatched in its size and splendour. The temple, with its massive gateways, its paintings of Shiva and the monolith of Shiva's steed, the Nandi bull, is an invaluable cultural legacy of the Chola kingdom.

The temple complexes became small townships where daily life and religious rituals were entwined. By the 13th century, the kingdom was in decline, and the dynasty ended in 1279.

TEMPLE OF SRIRANGAM

An interesting legend surrounds the temple of Srirangam, the largest and among the grandest temples in India. It is dedicated to the Hindu god Vishnu, who is enshrined in the temple reclining on a massive serpent. It is said that while the sage Vibhisana was carrying an idol of Vishnu to Sri Lanka, he placed it on the ground for a few minutes in Tiruchirappali to rest. When he tried to pick it up, it appeared stuck to the ground. Thus, a temple came up on that site.

The Chera Dynasty (800–1300)

The Chera kingdom extended over the Malabar Coast, Karur, Coimbatore and Salem, in present-day Kerala and Tamil Nadu. The dynasty was founded by Perumchottu Utiyan Cheralatan in the 9th century, but it was his son, Imayavaramban Nedum Cheralatan, who made the kingdom powerful and extended its reach in southern India. Kadalpirakottiya Vel Kelu Kuttuvan, mentioned in the great Tamil epic *Silappadigaram*, is considered the greatest Chera ruler.

The unique matrilineal family structure of the Nair class prevalent in Kerala came into existence during the Chera rule. Under this system, the wife and daughter inherited the family property, instead of the son. Trade with Persia, Arabia and even China thrived during the Chera reign with textiles, perfumes, camphor and even elephants being exported. The dynasty lasted until the 12th century, when the Hoysalas emerged, and power shifted from the Kerala and Tamil Nadu region to present-day Karnataka.

The Pandya Dynasty and Vijayanagara

The Pandyas occupied the present-day Madurai and Thirunelveli districts in Tamil Nadu, and a part of old Travancore. They were skilled in trade and grew in prosperity and influence to become the dominant southern power in the 13th century. Madurai was the capital of the kingdom and the centre of Tamil culture. Poetry received royal patronage in the Pandyan kingdom, and numerous assemblies of poets were held in Madurai to promote this literary pursuit. The earliest Tamil grammatical treatise, *Tolkappiyam*, is believed to have been written during the Pandyan reign.

The Pandyan supremacy was shortlived. Attacked by Turkish armies in the 14th century, the Pandyas were finally absorbed by the Vijayanagara Empire, renowned for the development of music, art and literature during its rule. Vijayanagar (City of Victory), in present-day Karnataka, was the capital of the empire that lasted from 1336–1565, reaching its peak of wealth and power during the reign of Krishna Deva Raya (1509–1529). The city was built around the original religious centre of the Virupaksha temple at Hampi, now a UNESCO World Heritage Site.

BROTHERS HARIHARA AND BUKKA RAYA

The origin of the Vijayanagara Empire is under debate. One theory suggests that it was established by two brothers, Harihara and Bukka Raya. They were taken prisoner by Muhammad bin Tughlaq of the Tughlaq dynasty, who ruled the Delhi Sultanate in the 14th century. The brothers converted to Islam while in custody. Later they were sent to the south to quell a rebellion and took the opportunity to seize the territory and establish their supremacy over it. They then converted back to Hinduism.

MUSLIMS INVADE INDIA

The earliest Muslim invasion of India took place in the 8th century when an Iraqi-Arab army conquered Sind, in present-day Pakistan, and extended its authority to western Punjab. The Rajputs were successful in resisting the invaders and prevented their expansion into northern India. However, a new onslaught from the Arabs was mounted in 997 by Mahmud of Ghazni, the son of a Turkish slave who became king of Ghazni, in present-day Afghanistan.

Mahmud of Ghazni (r. 997–1030)

Mahmud, who ascended the throne at the age of 27, led 17 raids into India in as many years, looting Indian cities of their gold, jewels and other treasures. His soldiers destroyed temples and murdered the local people in wanton acts of aggression. His early campaigns took place in Punjab and north-eastern India; towards the end, he attacked Somnath in the western state of Gujarat. The attack on the Somnath temple was particularly brutal, with hundreds of people crushed under the feet of elephants or taken as slaves. The temple itself, an architectural masterpiece with 14 domes and a majestic Shiva idol, was destroyed by the invaders and its cache of gold was looted. Mahmud of Ghazni succeeded in bringing Punjab and north-western India under Muslim rule. He used the immense wealth he had amassed from the plundered Indian cities to enrich his kingdom of Ghazni. He developed it into a major centre of art and culture, built mosques and palaces, set up colleges and laid out gardens. Mahmud of Ghazni died in 1030, spending the last years of his life warding off Central Asian tribes threatening his prosperous kingdom.

Muhammad of Ghur (r. 1175–1206)

Mahmud of Ghazni's descendants of the Ghaznavid dynasty ruled over a weakened kingdom until 1150, when 'Ala' al-Din Husayn of Ghur overthrew the dynasty. 'Ala' al-Din's nephew, Mu'izz al-Din Muhammad, known as Muhammad of Ghur, launched invasions into India in 1175. He conquered Punjab and Sind, but met resistance from the Rajputs when he reached Rajasthan. Rajput chief's Prithviraj Chauhan won the first battle against the forces of Muhammad of Ghur at Tarain in 1191 but suffered defeat during the second onslaught at Panipat the following year. With this victory, the Muslim forces were able to capture a large part of northern India, including Delhi. After Muhammad of Ghur was assassinated in Lahore in 1206, one of his generals, Lieutenant Qutb-ud-din Aibak declared himself the ruler of the Indian empire. The seat of his power was at Lahore, but later he shifted his capital to Delhi. A former Turkish slave, Qutb-ud-din Aibak founded the Mamluk (Slave) Dynasty, and with it the Delhi Sultanate came into being.

THE DELHI SULTANATE 1206–1526

Mamluk (Slave) Dynasty (1206–1290)

The Delhi Sultanate refers to the various Muslim dynasties, beginning with the Mamluk (Slave) dynasty, which ruled India from 1206 to 1526. The dynasties that succeeded the Slave dynasty include the Khilji (1290–1320), Tughlaq (1320–1413), Sayyid (1414–1450) and Lodhi (1451–1526). The

Sultanate had a total of 35 rulers from its beginning in the 13th century to its decline in the 16th century.

Qutb-ud-din Aibak of the Slave dynasty was the first sultan of Delhi and is best known for building the famous Qutb Minar monument and the Qutb-ud-din mosque in Delhi. Qutb-ud-din's formal tenure as ruler lasted only four years, cut short by his accidental death while playing polo. Qutb-ud-din was a pious Muslim who was called

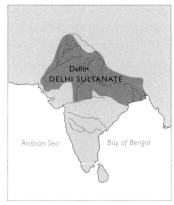

The Dehli Sultanate

Lakh Baksh or 'giver of hundred thousands' for his generous nature. His son, Aram Shah, was the sultan for a year but proved to be incompetent. After a succession struggle, Qutb-ud-din's son-in-law Iltutmish took over the reins of power.

Iltutmish (1210–1235), his daughter Raziya Sultan (1237-1240) who ruled for four years after him, and Balban (1266-1287) were the dynasty's most distinguished rulers. During the reign of Sultan Iltutmish, a permanent capital was established at Delhi and political ties with Ghur, in Afghanistan, were severed. Iltutmish also consolidated the power of the kingdom, retrieved lost territories and added new areas such as Malwa, in present-day Madhya Pradesh. Raziya Sultan, the only Muslim woman to rule India, was a just ruler and a skilled warrior who rode at the head of her army in battle. However, she was resented by her own people for being female and was murdered by one of her own palace guards.

Sultan Balban, considered the greatest military ruler of the Slave dynasty, was a strong administrator who ruled with an iron hand. His accomplishments included introducing a code of conduct at his court and building a strong army and defence structure, with numerous forts, in the kingdom. This helped protect the kingdom from the invading Mongols and other enemies. The power of the Slave dynasty diminished after Balban's death and a succession of weak leaders. Uprisings and revolts by the nobles of the kingdom plunged the administration into chaos and confusion until

Jalal-ud-din Khilji of the Afghan Khilji tribe seized power in 1290. Thus began the reign of the Khilji Dynasty in the Delhi Sultanate.

QUTB MINAR

The Qutb Minar, literally meaning 'axis minaret', was built in memory of the saint Qutb-ud-din Ushi, who is buried close by. It measures 16 m at its base and is 79 m tall. It has five storeys, each marked by a projecting balcony. The tower was built in three stages. Sultan Qutb-ud-din Aibak completed the first storey while the second, third and fourth storeys were completed by his successor and son-in-law, Iltutmish, in 1230. The Qutb Minar was damaged in 1368 when it was struck by lightning. The fallen top storey was replaced by two storeys, the fourth and the fifth, in 1370 by Feroz Shah Tughlaq (1351–1388).

The Khilji Dynasty (1290–1320)

Jalal-ud-din expanded the boundaries of his empire and was successful in suppressing the *thuggees* network of hoodlums engaged in murdering and robbing travellers in his kingdom during his six-year reign. When he despatched his nephew, Ala-ud-din, on a military campaign in southern India, Ala-ud-din hatched a conspiracy to fulfil his own ambitions. He obtained great wealth from his raids and, upon his return, murdered his uncle and became the sultan.

Ala-ud-din, who ruled from 1296 to 1316, was the most notorious of the Khilji sultans. He was an arrogant king who crushed the Hindus and established a network of spies to monitor discontent among the people. He successfully repelled Mongol invasions during his reign and tightened control of northern and central India. In 1307, he sent his general, Malik Kafur, to south India on a military campaign that resulted in the defeat of the major Deccan kingdoms. The Khilji Dynasty came to an end in 1320 with the death of the third and last Khilji sultan, Qutb-ud-din Mubarak Shah. Qutb-ud-din abolished the spy network and raised military wages, but was unable to secure his throne. His rule was marked by unrest, and eventually one of his own officers, Ghiyas ud-din Tughlaq, wrested power and established the Tughlaq dynasty in Delhi.

The Tughlaq Dynasty (1320–1413)

Ghiyas ud-din Tughlaq's reign was marked by political unrest and the constant threat of Mongol invasion from the north-western border. To fortify his kingdom, he built the mighty Tughlaqabad Fort, an architectural marvel in its time, though it now stands in ruins. The fort was part of Tughlaqabad, the third city of Delhi, and served as a defensive structure as well as the imperial capital of Ghiyas ud-din Tughlaq.

The Tughlaqabad Fort, with double-storied bastions and massive towers housing palaces, mosques and audience halls, was completed in four years. The city lies on the eastern outskirts of the fort and the tomb of Ghiyas ud-din Tughlaq, built by the ruler himself, is on the southern side. In 1325, when the fort was completed, Ghiyas ud-din Tughlaq died unexpectedly in an accident. He was succeeded by his son, Muhammad bin Tughlaq, a visionary under whose rule the kingdom expanded deep into the south. His empire stretched from Peshawar in the north and Madurai in the south, to Sind in the west and Assam in the east. The capital was transferred from Delhi to Devagiri, but was moved back after two years for the lack of facilities at Devagiri.

Muhammad bin Tughlaq died in 1351 of illness while trying to suppress a revolt in Gujarat. His cousin, Firuz Shah, who was the third Sultan of the Tughlaq dynasty, introduced reforms in the field of irrigation and the currency system, and built numerous gardens and parks in the Sultanate. The Tughlaq dynasty began to decline in 1398 when Mongol ruler Timur captured Tughlaqabad and plundered Delhi.

PAGLA TUGHLAQ

Muhammad bin Tughlaq earned the title Pagla Tughlaq for his numerous administrative and military blunders, and for his hare-brained schemes such as introducing copper and brass coins as currency that led to wide-scale forgery—the coins eventually had to be withdrawn.

The Sayyid and Lodhi Dynasties

The Delhi Sultanate broke up after the Timur invasion and the provinces declared their independence. Delhi saw a succession of rulers from the ranks of the nobles until 1414 when Khizr Khan founded the Sayyid dynasty and assumed control of the Sultanate. The 15th century saw two dynasties at the helm of the Delhi Sultanate—the Afghan Sayyids who ruled for 30 years until 1448, followed by the Lodhis.

The Lodhi dynasty was founded by Afghan noble Bahlul Lodhi in 1451. The Lodhis restored Delhi's supremacy over north India and there was peace in the region until Lodhi Sultan Ibrahim (1517–1526) antagonised his nobles when he tried to introduce laws curbing their power. Daulat Khan Lodhi, the governor of Punjab, rebelled and asked Kabul ruler Babur for help. Babur, who was a descendant of Mongol leaders Timur and Genghis Khan, welcomed the opportunity to invade the Sultanate. He met Ibrahim's huge army at Panipat, near Delhi, in 1526. His men were outnumbered, but with the power of muskets and artillery, used by an Islamic conqueror for the first time in the Indian subcontinent, he succeeded in killing Ibrahim and capturing Delhi. Babur's conquest signalled the end of the Delhi Sultanate and the start of the Mughal Empire in India. Mughal is the Persian word for Mongol and means 'tycoon'.

GENGHIS KHAN AND TIMUR

The Delhi Sultanate was threatened by Mongol invasions during the greater part of its existence, first from Genghis Khan in 1219, and two centuries later by his descendant, Timur or Tamerlane. It was in 1206 that Genghis Khan began his ambitious campaign to subjugate the world and invaded Pakistan. His son continued his policy of conquest, taking over Lahore and much of Pakistan and Afghanistan. From the 1240s, the Mongols made annual excursions into northern India and systematically plundered its treasures. Two centuries later, Timur tried to resurrect the Mongol Empire of Genghis Khan and conquered vast territories in Central Asia and Russia. He invaded Delhi in 1398, looting the city and killing thousands. His invasion sounded the death knell for the Tughlaq Dynasty which collapsed.

THE MUGHAL EMPIRE 1526–1858

The Mughals, descendants of the Mongols, ruled India for about three centuries, leaving behind a rich political and cultural legacy. Their reign was marked by a number of remarkable monarchs who made a significant contribution to India's art, architecture, customs, education, religious beliefs and governance. The empire had its share

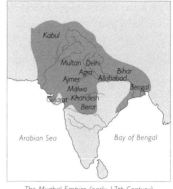

The Mughal Empire (early 17th Century)

of political machinations, rebellions and anarchy, but unlike the disparate dynasties of the Delhi Sultanate, the Mughal dynasty oversaw a period of relative peace, stability and prosperity. It began with Babur, reached its height under his grandson, Akbar, and ended with Bahadur Shah II in 1858.

Babur the Tiger (r. 1526–1530)

Babur was a military genius who captured Delhi in 1526 and set about conquering the Rajput kingdoms in the Gangetic Plains. In 1527, he conquered a Rajput confederacy led by Rana Sangha with a decisive defeat and routed the joint forces of the Afghans and the Sultan of Bengal two years later. By the end of his military campaigns, he had become the new sovereign of India.

Babur was a man of learning and refinement who wrote poetry and was passionate about landscaped gardens, creating several in Kabul, Lahore and Agra. He was a tolerant ruler who made peace with the southern kingdoms and allowed new Hindu temples to be built. One of his first acts as monarch was to abolish cow slaughter since it was offensive to Hindus. Trade with the rest of the Islamic world, especially Persia, and through Persia with Europe, was encouraged during his regime. Babur spent his last years, before his death at the age of 48, writing his autobiography, *Babur-Namah*, a candid, poetic account of his illustrious life. It is said that when his son, Humayun, fell seriously ill, Babur asked God to take his life and spare his son's. Humayun, as it turned out, made a complete recovery while Babur died a few days later.

Humayun (1530–1539, 1555–1556)

Babur was succeeded by Humayun who proved to be an inept ruler, lacking the political wisdom of his father. In 1539, he lost the empire his father had conquered to Afghan noble Sher Shah and went into exile in Iran. In 1555, Sher Shah's empire collapsed and Humayun returned to Delhi to restore the power of the Mughal dynasty. However, he ruled for only six months before he broke his neck during a fall and died. Humayun's tomb, located in Delhi, has the distinction of being the first of its kind, built in a garden setting. It is listed as a World Heritage Site.

Akbar the Great (1556–1605)

Akbar, Humayun's son and successor, is regarded as the greatest ruler of the Mughal Empire. Akbar was only aged 13 when he became the head of the powerful Mughal Empire after the sudden death of his father. He went on to rule the empire for 49 years. With the able guidance of his guardian, Bairam Khan, the young Akbar expanded the empire by conquering Gujarat, Bengal, Kashmir, Sind and Rajasthan. He developed a system of autonomy to rule the imperial provinces and placed military governors in every region. According to this system, the Hindu territories were under the control of the emperor but still largely independent—the British used the same model of governance when they took over India in the 18th and 19th centuries. Akbar also allowed Hindus to use their own law, rather than Islamic law, to regulate themselves.

To foster good relations with the Hindu-ruled kingdoms, he married Rajput princesses, and is believed to have had over 5,000 wives. His favourite wife was a Hindu and the mother of his successor, Jahangir. He also placed Hindus in key positions in his administration to unify Hindus and Muslims in the empire. In a radical move in 1564, Akbar abolished the hated *jizya* tax levied on non-Muslims; he had removed the pilgrimage tax paid by Hindus travelling to pilgrimage sites the preceding year.

Akbar believed in freedom of worship and religious tolerance, and tried to find a unifying element in all the faiths that were practised in his kingdom. He sponsored debates at his court between Christians, Hindus, Zoroastrians and Jains, and eventually broke away from conventional Islam and came up with a new religion, Din-i Ilahi or 'The Religion of God'. The religion was based on Islam and contained aspects of Jainism, Zoroastrianism and Hinduism: from Jainism, it took the principle of respect and care for all living things, while borrowing the Zoroastrian concept of sun worship and divine kingship. The religion died with Akbar in 1605.

Shunning Agra, Akbar built the sandstone city of Fatehpur Sikri (City of Victory) as the new capital of his kingdom. However, he abandoned Fatehpur Sikri after just 14 years because of problems with the water supply. The city remains in good condition even today, constituting a significant legacy of Akbar's rule. Located west of Agra in Uttar Pradesh, it is a synthesis of Hindu and Muslim architecture. It holds a mosque, a palace, sprawling gardens, public buildings, bath houses, a worship hall for Din-i Ilahi and a tomb for Akbar's religious advisor, Shaykh Salim Chishti. Akbar was particularly indebted to Chishti because he foretold the birth of the Mughal emperor's first son.

Art, particularly miniature paintings, blossomed under Akbar's patronage, as did music. Singer Mian Tansen, who created classical North Indian music for Akbar, was one of the nine gems of his court, and a particular favourite. Birbal who specialised in wit and humour, was another gem of Akbar's court.

AN ILLITERATE CONNOISSEUR OF LITERATURE

Akbar never formally learned to read or write but was a connoisseur of literature. Hindi literature grew in popularity, with Tulsi Das being one of the most celebrated Hindi writers of that period. Sanskrit texts were studied extensively and translated into Persian. Akbar also established numerous institutions of learning throughout his kingdom, notably in Delhi, Agra and Lahore.

Jahangir (r. 1605–1627)

Akbar was succeeded by his son, Jahangir, who reinstated Islam as the state religion while continuing Akbar's policy of religious tolerance. Jahangir did not pursue military conquest as forcefully as his father, but he did manage to assert Mughal rule over Bengal in eastern India. Jahangir's tenure is considered the richest period of Mughal culture, and he is best remembered for the magnificent monuments, buildings and gardens he built. His reign was also a period of opulence with luxurious palaces, lavish festivities and processions of silk-caparisoned elephants. Jahangir, known to be both tender and brutal, loved nature and art and lavished money on both. Along with his favourite wife, Nur Jahan, he patronised the arts and encouraged artists to create a unique Mughal style of miniature painting. Nur Jahan took charge of many of the palace affairs while Jahangir indulged in his pleasures, such as drinking *arrack*, a local alcoholic brew laced with opium. When Jahangir died in 1627, it was Nur Jahan's son, Shah Jahan, who ascended the throne.

Shah Jahan: the Emperor who Built The Taj Mahal (r. 1627–1658)

Shah Jahan's biggest legacy is the magnificent buildings he built, notably the Taj Mahal, the Agra Fort and the Red Fort. His opulent golden, jewel-encrusted throne was known as the Peacock Throne, named after its canopy held by 12 pillars decorated with peacocks.

Shah Jahan was also as keen on conquest as his ancestors; the empire began to expand once more during his reign. As part of his military pursuits, he quelled a Muslim rebellion in Ahmadnagar defended by Maratha noble Shaji Bhonsle, and annexed the territory. He also tried to destabilise the Deccan sultanates of Bijapur and Golconda by creating trouble between the Maratha chieftains and the sultans. Shah Jahan was responsible for shifting the seat of power from Agra back to Delhi.

Shah Jahan was devastated by the death of his beloved wife, Mumtaz Mahal, in 1631, during the birth of their 14th child. Thereafter, he devoted all his time to building monuments across the kingdom, notably, the world-famous Taj Mahal. Located in Agra, this mausoleum to his wife was started in 1632 and took almost 20 years to complete. Shah Jahan also built Shahjahanabad, the area that is present-day Old Delhi, which was the seat of Mughal power in Delhi. Shahjahanabad holds the Red Fort and the Jama Masjid, the largest mosque in India.

The Red Fort, built of massive blocks of sandstone, took ten years to complete. It consists of public and private halls, marble palaces, a mosque and lavish gardens. Despite attacks by the Persian Emperor Nadir Shah in 1739, and by British soldiers in 1857, the Red Fort still stands as a striking symbol of Mughal rule in Delhi.

TAJ MAHAL

Shah Jahan is best known for the exquisite Taj Mahal, his labour of love for his late wife, Mumtaz Mahal. It took 20,000 labourers to complete the marble structure that is set in a Persian landscaped garden on the banks of the Yamuna River. The site was selected because of its location on a bend in the river, so that it could be seen from Shah Jahan's palace at the Agra Fort. Shah Jahan engaged labourers and artisans, and sourced marble, sandstone and semiprecious stones used for the marble inlay work from all over India and abroad. The pure white marble came from Makrana in Rajasthan, crystal and jade from China, lapis lazuli and sapphires from Sri Lanka, carnelian from Baghdad and turquoise from Tibet. The master mason came from Baghdad.

The Taj Mahal is made up of four minarets surrounding a central dome. An ornate marble screen, finely carved to produce the appearance of lace, surrounds the cenotaph in the central hall. The actual graves of Mumtaz Mahal and Shah Jahan lie in an underground crypt directly below the cenotaphs. The white monument reflects the changing light of the day, dazzling one minute, glowing the next and shimmering in the moonlight.

Aurangzeb: the Last of the Great Mughal Rulers (r. 1658–1707)

Shah Jahan fell ill in 1658 and was imprisoned by his son Aurangzeb in Agra shortly afterwards. Aurangzeb then executed his elder brother and captured the throne, declaring himself as the ruler of the vast Mughal Empire. Shah Jahan died a few years later in 1666.

Aurangzeb, the last of the illustrious Mughal rulers, expanded the empire to its fullest extent. He seized the southern kingdoms of Golconda and Bijapur and captured all the territories held by the Marathas who continued to resist using guerrilla warfare tactics. He eventually established a state in the Western Ghat region in south-west India, in present-day Maharashtra.

Aurangzeb was a pious Muslim who ended the policy of religious tolerance advocated by his ancestors. He insisted that the *sharia* (Islamic law) be followed by everyone and he reimposed the *jizya* tax on non-Muslims that Akbar had abolished. He also introduced a new custom duty and levied a higher rate of tax on non-Muslims, creating considerable unrest among Hindus. A staunch Muslim, Aurangzeb forbade drinking and gambling in his empire and imposed Islam on his subjects. He was responsible for crushing a Hindu religious sect, the Satnamis, and beheading the ninth guru of Sikhism, Tegh Bahadur. The Sikhs, religious reformers who turned militant under the Mughals, revolted against Aurangzeb's rule and continued their hostilities towards the empire. By the early 1800s, they had succeeded in carving out an independent kingdom with the capital at Lahore.

Among other unpopular moves, Aurangzeb withdrew lavish state support of the arts although he continued to patronise intellectuals and architects whose works—such as the Pearl Mosque in Delhi—were related to Islam. However, he destroyed hundreds of Hindu temples and other non-Muslim places of worship during his rule of terror.

Aurangzeb died in 1707 at the age of 88, leaving a Mughal empire weakened by growing unrest among Muslims and Hindus, constant conflict and a depleted treasury. One of his four sons, Bahadur Shah I, took over control of the empire but it never regained its past glory. The subsequent Mughal emperors were ineffectual puppet leaders who merely had a nominal presence. By the time Ahmad Shah took over the Mughal throne in 1748, the power of the empire was all but extinguished. India was divided into regional states which, while recognising the nominal supremacy of the Mughals, wielded considerable power and influence. The Mughal Empire officially came to an end in 1858 when the last ruler, Bahadur Shah II, was deposed by the British and exiled to Burma.

THE RISE OF THE MARATHAS

The first major threat to Aurangzeb's authority came from the Marathas, a powerful group of warriors operating in the Western Ghat region, in present-day Maharashtra, under Shivaji Bhonsle. Shivaji instilled patriotism and devotion to Hinduism in his people and inspired them to rebel against Aurangzeb's tyrannical policies. Against all odds, the indomitable Shivaji established a Hindu kingdom in 1674 and declared himself Chatrapati or the King. He extended his territory to claim Nasik and Poona in the east and Vellore and Tanjore in the south. Shivaji died at the age of 53 and was succeeded by his son Shambaji, who was captured and killed by Aurangzeb. Despite their setbacks, the subsequent Maratha leaders remained steadfast in their goal of a Maratha homeland and continued to rebel against the Mughals, as well as British imperialism at a later stage.

In the early 18th century, power passed to the Peshwas, who were prime ministers under the descendants of Shivaji. Nana Saheb was a Peshwa who became one of the most powerful rulers in India, with an empire that extended from the Deccan to Gujarat, Rajasthan and Punjab. He died shortly after the Third Battle of Panipat when Afghan armies led by Ahmad Shah Durrani defeated the Marathas. The Maratha power declined after this battle and was further crippled by the British, led by Mountstuart Elphinstone, who occupied the office of Resident (Pune) in 1811. Maratha leader Bajirao II finally submitted to the British on 3 June 1818, signalling the end of the glory of Maratha power.

THE ARRIVAL OF THE EUROPEANS

Trade in spices, cotton, silk and other goods played a key role in relations between India and other countries in ancient times. By the 1st century, it had expanded substantially because of advances in transport. Pack animals were used to transport goods over land along the designated spice and silk routes, while sturdy vessels were used for the sea.

At the turn of the century, trade between India and the ancient Roman Empire and the Parthian Empire was extensive. Wealthy Romans bought spices, cloth and even live animals and birds from India in exchange for gold coins. In subsequent years, Indian goods also found their way to Western nations such as Italy, via the Arab lands, China and South-east Asia. Interest in Indian goods prompted the Europeans to travel to India in the 15th and 16th centuries to net lucrative trading opportunities. The Portuguese were the first Europeans to land by sea in India at the end of the 15th century. They were forced to find an alternate route to India after the traditional trade routes were closed by the Ottoman Empire. The Dutch, French and British came later, attracted by the prospect of huge profits to be made in India. Trade with these European companies enriched kingdoms such as Bengal and Bihar, which were independent of the weakened Mughal Empire.

The Portuguese Traders

Portuguese sailor Vasco da Gama took a circuitous route around Africa, crossing the Cape of Good Hope in South Africa to land at the western Indian port city of Calicut, Kerala, in May 1498 to trade in precious Indian spices. The goods he took back to Lisbon brought him a huge profit, which inspired others to make the trip to India. A second Portuguese expedition led by Pedro Alvares Cabral travelled to India a few years later and set up a trading post in Cochin. Soon the Portuguese had trading posts all along the west coast and controlled the entire trade in the Indian Ocean.

Franciso-de-Almedia was the first governor of Portuguese affairs in India and led the Portuguese colonising efforts until Alfanso-de-Albuquerque, the commander of a squadron, was appointed governor in 1509. Alfanso-de-Albuquerque was a capable leader who consolidated Portugal's position in India. Shortly after taking over as governor, he captured Goa from the Bijapur Sultanate and made it the Portuguese seat of power in India.

After Alfanso's death in 1515, his successors brought Diu, Daman and Bombay into the Portuguese fold. However, the Portuguese desire to make quick profits and their zeal in spreading Christianity worked against them. The local people, forced to embrace Christianity after the arrival of Spanish priest Francis Xavier in 1542, rebelled against the foreign colonisers and weakened their hold in India. The Portuguese were also unable to compete with the other Europeans who had landed in India looking for lucrative trading opportunities. The Portuguese gradually lost all their territories, except for Diu, Daman and Goa, which they retained until 1961.

Trade Wars

Following the example of the Portuguese, Dutch merchants, who had set up their East India Company in the region, arrived in India in search of trade in the early 17th century. They established their first trading post near Chennai, venturing further afield along the western coast right up to Bengal.

In 1616, the Dutch set up a printing press in Serampore, Bengal, and opened Protestant missions there. But their real interest lay in the East Indies where they found it more profitable to trade in spices. They slowly gave up their possessions in India to concentrate on this region.

The French also made inroads into India for commercial purposes. They established a factory in Surat, Gujarat, and their first trading post at Pondicherry in the south in 1664. The French, under Joseph Francois Dupleix, went on an expansionist drive and acquired Karaikal, Yanam and Mahe in the south and Chandannagar near Calcutta in the east. The three southern enclaves and the town of Pondicherry together form the modern union territory of Pondicherry.

The French struggled for trading supremacy with the British during the greater part of the 18th century. The two countries were bitter rivals and entered local power struggles, particularly in the southern kingdoms where they helped install rulers friendly to their interests. Their rivalry in India was a prelude to the worldwide Seven Years War (1756–1763) that the two European powers were involved in. Ultimately the British, led by Lieutenant Colonel Robert Clive, were victorious in India. However, they returned Pondicherry to the French, and it remained a district of France until 1954 when the Indian government took over its administration. Chandannagar was incorporated in West Bengal state in 1949.

The British East India Company (1608–1858)

The British East India Company was set up in 1600 by a group of merchants to facilitate trade with Asia. Its main target was the East Indies, but the British were unable to break the Dutch stranglehold on the spice trade there and turned their attention to India instead. The company arrived in India in 1608, lured by the spices, silks, jewels and the cheap labour available. It set up a chain of factories all over the country and, by the middle of the 18th century, had overtaken its rivals to become a major commercial entity, reaping huge profits. Much of its success was achieved through plunder and manipulation.

The company was initially not interested in conquest, but when its power and influence grew, it brought in soldiers to defend itself from the harassment of local princes. It also began to intervene in Indian politics to enhance its profits and secure its possessions. The turning point in the company's affairs in India came when company troops defeated a rebellious prince at the Battle of Plassey in 1757 and the British East India Company became the ruler of Bengal. Another significant event was the Battle of Buxar in 1764 in which the British company defeated a group of Indian princes. Under Lieutenant Colonel Robert Clive, the company indulged in large-scale plunder, extortion and atrocities against anyone who rebelled against its rule. As its political and commercial power grew, it set out to expand its territorial acquisitions.

TIPU SULTAN: THE TIGER OF MYSORE

Tipu Sultan was the Muslim ruler of the southern kingdom of Mysore, who posed a serious threat to the rapidly spreading power and influence of the British East India Company. Mysore was involved in four wars with the British, and Tipu fought in all four, first under his father Haider Ali and later as the sultan of Mysore after his father died. He was killed by the British in May 1799 while defending his capital Seringapatam during the Fourth Mysore War.

Concerned about the atrocities and exploitative practices of the company, the British government recalled Clive. It tightened its control on the company by appointing Warren Hastings as governor general of Bengal in charge of affairs in India. In other changes brought about by the British government, parliamentary acts of 1813 and 1833 ended the company's trade monopoly. It also banned discrimination against Indians who were in government employment.

The new British governor generals instituted a variety of reforms in India. Lord William Bentinck, who was governor general from 1828 to 1835, abolished *sati*, the practice of widow self-immolation, and banned *thuggees*, armed gangs who robbed and killed travellers. Widow remarriage was allowed by law and the ancient *Devadasi* tradition, in which women were 'married' to temple deities and trained in dance and music to entertain the Lord was banned. English was made the official language of the country and a number of Christian missionary schools and institutions of higher learning were built to provide English education.

Lord Dalhousie, as governor general, had roads and irrigation systems constructed and founded the Post and Telegraph Department. He made radical changes in Hindu law, terminating the right of an Indian ruler to adopt his heir. This change in law was widely unpopular, as it resulted in a number of independent states, including Jhansi, coming under the control of the British. The territories annexed by the company formed British India, which was divided into provinces such as Madras, Bengal and Bombay, and subdivided into districts. Governors, councillors, district collectors and other officials in these provinces were part of the Indian Civil Service (ICS) introduced by Lord Cornwallis when he was governor general. Indians were not allowed in the ICS until the 1860s. The states that were not under direct British rule retained their own monarchs but were required to follow the orders of the British. Calcutta became the capital of the British East India Company's Indian territories.

RANI OF JHANSI

Lakshmi Bai, or Rani of Jhansi, the queen of the kingdom of Jhansi, was one of the heroines of the nationalist movement. She became a widow at the age of 18 after the death of her husband, Maharaja Gangadhar Rao, on 21 November 1853. The British refused to accept the Maharaja's adopted son as his heir and decided to annex Jhansi. Lakshmi Bai, determined to defend her kingdom, assembled an army of volunteers and fought fearlessly when the British invaded Jhansi in March 1858. Despite her best efforts, she was defeated but she managed to escape dressed as a man with her son strapped to her back. The British caught up with her in neighbouring Gwalior and she died fighting on 18 June 1858. She was just 22 years old.

The company required more revenue to sustain its expansionist policies as British India grew in size. For this purpose, it taxed the public heavily and asked for more tribute from the independent states. This caused widespread public discontent and unrest, which in turn limited the growth of the economy. In 1857, unhappy Indian troops in Bengal revolted against British rule. In 1858, the British government dissolved the British East India

Company and assumed direct control of its Indian affairs, paving the way for the British Raj.

THE SIKHS AND THE KOHINOOR DIAMOND

The Sikhs formed a powerful empire in Punjab during British company rule and were united under Ranjit Singh who was known as the 'Lion of Punjab'. Ranjit Singh was the chief of the Sukerchakia clan and established the Sikh kingdom of Punjab, after capturing Lahore in 1799. He built up a formidable army and gradually expanded the empire to include parts of Himachal Pradesh and Kashmir in the extreme north. The kingdom was inhabited by Sikhs, the dominant group, as well as by Hindus and Muslims. Ranjit Singh encouraged agriculture and supported commerce and industry in the state. His empire was peaceful and prosperous, and he enjoyed amicable relations with the British. After his death in 1839, the empire fell into disarray and six years later, in 1845, the Sikhs fought their first war with the British and had to give up part of their empire.

It was at this time that Maharaja Duleep Singh, a minor under the guardianship of his mother, gave away the famous Kohinoor (Mountain of Light) diamond to the British to adorn Queen Victoria's crown. The 106-carat diamond was acquired by Ranjit Singh as part of his booty during a military campaign in Afghanistan. Under Ranjit Singh's will, the diamond was to be given to a Hindu temple in Orissa. But his request was not carried out.

According to legend, the Kohinoor diamond originated in the diamond-producing region of Golconda in Andhra Pradesh. It belonged to the king of Malwa in the 14th century and fell into the hands of Muhammad bin Tughlaq in 1323. It later came under the possession of Mughal Emperor Babur but was plundered by Nadir Shah of Persia and taken to Afghanistan from where Ranjit Singh brought it to the Punjab. It is now on display at the Tower of London.

THE BRITISH RAJ

Sepoy Mutiny of 1857

The Indian mutiny of 1857, also known as the Sepoy Mutiny, was a significant milestone in the history of British rule in India. It brought an end to the corrupt and excessive practices of the British East India Company and marked the beginning of the direct rule of the British crown, referred to as the British Raj. The mutiny was triggered by pent-up resentment against the governance of the British East India Company. The common man was tired of the harsh land policies of Governor General Lord Dalhousie and his successor, Lord Canning, the steady expansion of the company holdings and the growing westernisation that threatened Indian culture.

The first spark occurred in the Bengal Army. Indian soldiers had a multitude of grievances, chief among them dissatisfaction with the denial of foreign service allowances and postings to Burma and other places outside India. The final trigger was the new rifle given to soldiers, which had a cardboard cartridge. Soldiers were required to bite off the end of the cartridge to load the rifle. When rumours began to spread that the waterproofing grease of the cartridge was made of beef or pork fat, making it religiously impure for both Hindus and Muslims, the soldiers refused to use the rifles. The British authorities allowed them to make their own waterproofing, but the rebellious mood persisted.

On 10 May 1857, 85 soldiers at the army camp in Meerut were imprisoned for refusing to use the new rifles. This angered the other soldiers who shot the British officers, took over the camp and marched to Delhi, where they proclaimed Mughal Emperor Bahadur Shah II as their leader. The mutineers were joined by other soldiers and Mughal nobles as the uprising spread to Haryana, Uttar Pradesh, Bihar and Madhya Pradesh, growing into a large-scale rebellion against British rule.

The Crown Takes Charge

The Sepoy Mutiny was confined to the northern part of the country where there was more dissatisfaction compared to Calcutta, Madras and Bombay, which had enjoyed a greater measure of prosperity under company rule. By the end of 1858, the rebellion was finally contained, the mutineers defeated and control wrested back by the British. Bahadur Shah II was exiled to Burma for supporting the mutineers and the Mughal Empire officially came to an end.

As a direct fallout of the mutiny, the British government dissolved the British company in India and assumed control of Indian affairs. It appointed a secretary of state for India who was chosen by the British prime minister and answerable to the British Parliament. His representative in India was the governor general who was given the title of viceroy. Queen Victoria was proclaimed Empress of India in 1876. The seat of power of the British Raj, as it was during the days of company rule, remained at Calcutta until 1911 when it was shifted to Delhi.

Society and Economy under British Rule

The British executed thousands of suspected rebels after quelling the mutiny, before turning its attention to the business of governing India. One of their immediate tasks was to woo back the educated and elite classes and the princely states. The princes received land and titles and guarantees that their states would not be annexed by the British. Rural leaders received judicial powers while members of the elite were made magistrates and knights in the cities.

To enhance internal security, the Indian Army began recruiting soldiers from communities such as the Sikhs and Punjabi Muslims who had helped them in their fight against the mutineers. Nonetheless, the British soldiers retained exclusive charge of the artillery, and their numbers were increased in India.

The British developed cantonments as secure, self-contained residential townships for their officials and their families. These communities had markets, churches, hospitals and houses for comfortable living. During the hot summer months, the British moved to the cooler hill stations such as Simla and Nainital, where they developed residential colonies. They indulged in sports, parties and picnics with the help of cheap domestic labour. The British influence produced a new breed of Indians, who were Indian in appearance but English in taste, mannerisms and the way they spoke. They were informally referred to as 'Brown Sahibs'.

The Indian economy, primarily dependent on agriculture, grew steadily during British rule. Over 70 per cent of the population worked in agriculture and reaped profits from the exports of raw cotton, jute, tea and grain. India supplied 20 per cent of Britain's wheat requirement and 59 per cent of its tea. Tea was grown mainly on British-owned plantations. By the 1890s, power looms were being installed in textile factories in Bombay and this became an important manufacturing industry in the country.

The growth of the economy was enhanced by the development of the railways, telegraph and cheap postal service. However, while landowners and businessmen grew affluent, the poorer classes received few benefits under the British and made little progress. Education reforms, which gained momentum by the 1920s, helped improve literacy in English and the Indian languages.

REFORM MOVEMENTS

The British had a major influence in the genesis of the reform movements in India. Knowledge of English and exposure to Western culture encouraged Indian intellectuals to form their own associations to reform society and shape religious beliefs and practices. While the foundation for these movements was laid in the early years of the 19th century, the movements gained momentum and expanded during the British Raj.

In 1875, reformer Swami Dayananda Saraswati, who propagated the belief in one all-knowing God while denouncing image worship, founded the Bombay Arya Samaj (Society of Aryans). The movement encouraged its followers to speak Hindi and adopt the ways of the *Vedas*. The Arya Samaj became very influential over the years and had almost two million followers by 1947.

Another successful movement was the Ramakrishna Mission founded in 1897 by Narendranath Datta, called Swami Vivekananda, to spread the message of social service and the teachings of the ancient Vedic scriptures, the *Upanishads*. The Sikhs formed their own Singh Sabha in 1873 to teach people about Sikhism and to win back Sikhs who had converted to other religions. These associations spread their messages in India as well as overseas, particularly in the West, where the Ramakrishna Mission had particular impact.

Caste-based associations were also formed during this period, and these groups lobbied the government to further their own interests and protect their members. One such group was the Non-Brahmin Movement which protested against the large number of Brahmins in government employment. These different forces laid the foundation for the rise of nationalism in India.

RAM MOHUN ROY

An eminent social and religious reformer of the early 19th century, Ram Mohun Roy was an intellectual who had a major impact on politics, public administration, the press and education. Roy is sometimes called the Father of Modern India for his significant contributions to the development of modern Indian society. He challenged the caste system and condemned social evils such as sati, polygamy and infanticide, while advocating a Hinduism devoid of idol worship, orthodox rituals and superstitions. Believing in one God—Brahma—Roy founded the Brahmo Samaj (Association of Brahma) to reform Hinduism and check the spread of Christianity. Roy went to Britain as an ambassador of the Mughal Empire in 1831 and died there of meningitis two years later.

RISE OF INDIAN NATIONALISM

Even as social and religious reform movements were gathering momentum in India, a nascent nationalism was taking root among young educated Indians from the upper and middle classes. Well versed in English and Western thought and ideas, they believed that they, and not the British, should be in control of India. One of the first nationalist groups to emerge was the Indian National Congress.

Indian National Congress

The Indian National Congress came into being in December 1885 with the aim of playing a role in the governing of India and pressuring the British-led government to bring about reforms and remedy the grievances of the public. Seventy-two people attended the first meeting of this new group of the Indian educated elite convened in Bombay. Subsequently, the party met every December in a different city. Its first president was Womesh Chandra Banerjee. The main organisers of the party present at the historic first meeting were Allan Octavian Hume, a British theosophist and retired officer of the ICS; Bombay lawyer Pherozeshah Mehta; and Surendranath Banerjea, a Bengali who was among the first Indians to pass the entrance examination for the ICS. Mehta and Banerjea were followers of London-based businessman and nationalist Dadabhai Naoroji.

The party started out by passing resolutions at its annual meetings, which the British tried to address. In response to the demands of the Congress, the government raised the age limit for the ICS examination to 23 and introduced indirect elections to the legislative councils. Dissension appeared in the ranks of the party in 1906 when a group of radical members, led by Bal Gangadhar Tilak, expressed opposition to the British division of Bengal on religious lines. The moderates were also opposed to the partition of Bengal but preferred to maintain good relations with the British so as to solve the dispute. By 1907, the party had split into two, with Tilak and his radicals, and the moderates led by Gopal Krishna Gokhale, going their separate ways. Tilak took an aggressive stance and instigated his followers to confront the British. This led to his arrest and enabled Gokhale to consolidate his position in the Congress party.

The Congress has produced some of the greatest leaders in modern Indian history, men and women who steered the country on the road to freedom and later governed it as an independent nation. Some of the illustrious Congress presidents after Gokhale were Dr Annie Besant, Maulana Abul Kalam Azad, Mahatma Gandhi, Sarojini Naidu, Pandit Jawaharlal Nehru, Sardar Vallabhbhai Patel and Dr Rajendra Prasad. Under Gandhi, the Congress, predominantly Hindu, became a mass organisation, with members from almost every religious, ethnic, economic and linguistic group. The party went on to form the first government in independent India in 1947. Dr Rajendra Prasad was India's first president and Pandit Jawaharlal Nehru its first prime minister.

The Muslim League

The Muslims, poorly represented in the Hindu-dominated Indian National Congress and anxious about Hindu domination, formed their own party, the All India Muslim League, in Dhaka in 1906. The party was modelled on the Congress, and its agenda was to safeguard the rights and liberties of Muslims in India. One of the party's main demands was that Muslims be allowed to vote separately from other Indians and to vote for their own candidates, so as to ensure adequate representation for their community. The League was based in Lucknow, and the Aga Khan was elected its first president.

The League took a moderate stand towards the British and supported their decision to partition Bengal. However, the British move to reunite the Bengali-speaking region in 1911, upon pressure from the Congress, angered League leaders. Muhammad Ali Jinnah became president of the League in 1916 and under his leadership, the party became a powerful force in Indian politics. By 1940, it was calling for the establishment of a Muslim state, despite opposition from the Indian National Congress. Jinnah got his way when Pakistan was formed in 1947 at the partition of the Indian subcontinent, and the Muslim League became the major political party of the newly formed country. Jinnah was appointed governor general, and another League leader, Liaquat Ali Khan, became the new prime minister. However, after Jinnah's death in September 1948 and Liaquat's assassination in October 1951, the League began to weaken. By 1953, it had disintegrated, and several different political parties had formed in its place.

World War I and Massacre at Jallianwala Bagh

Despite their promises, the British failed to give Indian leaders a greater share in government. They also failed to reward the loyalty and dedication with which Indian soldiers had fought for the Allies in France and the Middle East during World War I. Over a million Indian soldiers and labourers were involved in the Allied war effort, and as many as 60,000 were killed. Many Indians hoped that their wartime sacrifice would be rewarded with self-government similar to that enjoyed by the other British dominions such as Canada and Australia.

The war, however, heightened British insecurity. They were unwilling to concede to the demands for self-rule; but they made some concessions as recommended by Viceroy Lord Chelmsford and British Secretary of State Edwin Montagu. The Montagu-Chelmsford reforms changed the structure of the central and provincial governments by giving greater power and revenues to the provinces, as well as to the princes. But hopes for a better system of governance were dashed by the Rowlatt Acts, which gave the government more power to deal with seditious behaviour.

The Acts led to public outrage and protests. On Sunday, 13 April 1919, 10,000 people gathered at Jallianwala Bagh in Amritsar Punjab, to protest against the judicial regulations. The Hindu Baisakhi Spring Festival also fell on that day. The peaceful protest turned into a massacre when British officer General Dyer, without giving any warning, ordered his soldiers to fire into the crowd. For 10 to 15 minutes, 1,650 rounds of ammunition were fired into the crowd of unarmed men, women and children. According to official estimates, nearly 400 people were killed and another 1,200 were wounded.

Dyer was relieved of his command, but he returned to Britain a hero, and received a jewelled sword inscribed 'Saviour of the Punjab' from conservatives. The incident gave a fillip to the civil strife, turning millions of moderate Indians into nationalists. One such Indian was Mohandas Karamchand Gandhi, later known as Mahatma (Great Soul) Gandhi, who launched his historic revolutionary *satyagraha* (devotion to truth) movement against the British a year after the horrific Jallianwala Bagh massacre.

Mahatma Gandhi (1869–1948)

Mohandas Karamchand Gandhi is one of the most influential figures in modern Indian history. He has earned the title 'Father of the Nation' for the key role he played in India's freedom struggle. A lawyer by profession, he was born on 2 October 1869 into a family of merchants in Porbundar, Gujarat. He broke with tradition and went to the University College, London, to study law where he was inspired by Henry David Thoreau's book, *Civil Disobedience*, which sowed in him the seeds of non-violent protest that he used effectively to win freedom for India. He was also influenced by Russian writer Leo Tolstoy.

Gandhi returned to India in 1891 and later left for Durban, South Africa, where he was the first 'coloured' lawyer admitted to the bar. Horrified by the discrimination against non-whites that he saw there, he became a champion of Indian rights and founded the Natal Indian Congress. An attack by white South Africans drove him to launch a civil disobedience movement against the authorities. He received the support of thousands of Indians who went to jail with him.

When Gandhi returned to India in 1914, he joined the Indian National Congress and launched a campaign of social reform and non-cooperation with the British at the grassroots level. He formally entered Indian politics in April 1920 when he took over leadership of Annie Besant's Home Rule League. In 1921, he became president of the Congress Party. To spread his message of non-violence, non-cooperation and social reform, Gandhi travelled across the country, visiting villages and small towns in every state. He himself discarded his European clothes, preferring to wear the traditional Indian attire of *dhoti* (a long wrap-around garment worn at the midriff), shawl and sandals. With his shaven head and sparse clothing, he travelled in third class train compartments to identify with the poor.

During his visits, he urged the people to boycott the British government and courts, and spin their own cotton instead of using British-made cloth. British exploitation of Indian villagers had caused extreme poverty in rural areas and had virtually destroyed the local industries; developing Indian home industries was an important element in Gandhi's *Swaraj* (self-rule) movement.

Gandhi preached the benefits of non-violence, *satyagraha* and self-control. Gandhi was also a social reformer who championed the cause of women, equality of religion and dignity of labour. He was opposed to child marriage. He used hunger strikes, boycotts of foreign goods and refusal to pay taxes as tactics in his civil disobedience movement against the British. Gandhi's leadership galvanised the nationalists and brought an outpouring of support from Indians from all walks of life. However, the public did not always remain peaceful, and violence broke out on several occasions. In 1922, when a mob in Uttar Pradesh burned down a police station killing 22 constables inside, Gandhi called off his non-cooperation campaign. He was imprisoned shortly afterwards and stayed in jail for two years.

Gandhi's Salt March

Gandhi launched a new campaign of civil disobedience in March 1930, targetting the salt tax. Salt was a government monopoly and the public had to pay tax for the salt they bought. The sale or production of salt by anyone other than the British government was a crime punishable by law. In sheer defiance of the law, Gandhi asked people to produce their own salt from sea water in protest against the unfair tax. In a symbolic gesture, on 12 March, the 61-year-old Gandhi led a procession of 78 followers from Ahmedabad, Gujarat, to the town of Dandi on the Arabian Sea, about 400 km away. The journey took 23 days on foot. On 6 April, when they reached Dandi, Gandhi picked up a lump of mud and salt and boiled it in seawater to make salt. He urged his followers to make salt and sell it all along the coast. Gandhi was imprisoned for defying the salt law. Following the Salt March, Gandhi and the Congress launched other campaigns, notably the boycott of British imported goods, particularly cloth, in protest against the stifling of the Indian textile industry by British policies. Thousands of people were jailed and hundreds killed or injured by the British because of their involvement in Gandhi's non-cooperation movement. Gandhi was released from jail several months later and the British eventually conceded to some of his demands, such as allowing Indians to make untaxed salt for their own use.

Hindu-Muslim Differences

By 1932, the framework of a new constitution for India had been worked out in London. Under the new constitution, power was divided between the federal and provincial governments, with a prime minister heading each province. The different religious communities were accorded their own electorates.

The first provincial elections under the new constitution were held in 1937, and the Congress ended up winning in eight of the 11 provinces. The remaining three provinces—Bengal, Punjab and Sind—were controlled by regional parties.

The poor showing of the Muslim League during the elections caused concern among its leadership. President Jinnah was suspicious of the Congress and feared that Indian Muslims would become a minority in a democratic India. He was particularly concerned that Hindi was being promoted at the expense of Urdu by the new provincial governments, and that Hindus were treating their patriotic hymn *Vande Mataram* as the national anthem.

In March 1940, the Muslim League's concerns were made official when it passed a resolution at a party meeting in Lahore, stating that Muslims would have their own states in a free India where they would not be under Hindu rule. Jinnah and his followers began to speak of the north-east and north-west, where Muslims resided in large numbers, as a single Muslim state—Pakistan. Pakistan, meaning 'pure land', was a name created from the names of the Muslim states of the north-west: 'P' from Punjab, 'A' for the Afghan areas and 'K' for Kashmir.

The League saw rapid growth during the World War II years and became a mass party by 1945. By 1942 and 1943, after Jinnah had installed League members as provincial prime ministers in the provinces of Sind and Bengal, the League had control of a total of five provinces, including Assam, the North-west Frontier Province and Punjab, setting the foundation for the formation of Pakistan.

Quit India Movement

During World War II, the British promised Congress Party leaders that India would become independent if Indians supported the war. The Congress turned down the offer and demanded immediate independence, launching the Quit India Movement in August 1942 to press their demands; they were not granted by British Prime Minister Winston Churchill. Gandhi coined the slogan 'Quit India' and also issued a 'Do or Die' call at a speech during a rally on 8 August at the Gowalia Tank Maidan grounds in Bombay, renamed August Kranti Maidan (August Revolution Ground). In response to the speech, the British imprisoned the entire Congress leadership. Most of the Congress leaders spent the remaining years of World War II in jail. However, the campaign touched a raw nerve among the masses, particularly the rural poor suffering from the effects of the country's worst famine in 40 years. Angry peasants across the country showed their ire against the British by attacking police stations, post offices and other official facilities in the biggest rebellion since the mutiny of 1857. The uprising, which caused a collapse of government in many areas, was suppressed by mid-1943.

SUBHAS CHANDRA BOSE AND THE
INDIAN NATIONAL ARMY

A committed nationalist who was president of the Indian National Congress, Subhas Chandra Bose went overseas during World War II to garner support to oust the British from India. He formed the Provisional Government of Free India and mobilised overseas Indians, including members of the newly formed Indian National Army (INA), to bring about the expulsion of the British. INA, made up of prisoners of war and civilian residents of South-east Asia, launched its first attack to liberate India across the India-Burma border. INA units succeeded in besieging Imphal, in the north-east, before the British began their counter-offensive and took a large number of INA soldiers prisoner. Bose, called Netaji (leader) by his followers, was reportedly killed in an air crash over Taipei, Taiwan, on 18 August 1945, though there is no 'irrefutable proof' of his death.

At the end of World War II, the British had little interest left in India; they were busy getting their own house back in order. The stage was set for granting independence to India, but Viceroy Lord Wavell's challenge was to achieve a smooth transition to independence that would be acceptable to both the Congress and the Muslim League. The British proposed the creation of a self-governing Pakistan within a federal India, which was rejected by Congress leader Jawaharlal Nehru, as well as Jinnah who wanted a completely independent Pakistan. The stalemate instigated the Great Calcutta Killing, in which Hindus and Muslims fought violent street battles resulting in the death of 4,000 people. The communal violence spread to Bihar and Punjab. The British, keen to broker a peaceful solution to the communal crisis, replaced Wavell with Lord Mountbatten. The Congress leaders finally capitulated and in April 1947 informed Mountbatten of their decision to accept an independent Pakistan. Of the princely states, except for Hyderabad and Kashmir, the rest acceded to India. Pakistan was formed with part of Bengal and Punjab.

On 14 August 1947, Pakistan became an independent nation while India was declared independent from British rule at midnight on 15 August.

Jinnah was the first governor general of the new Republic of Islamic Pakistan. Jawaharlal Nehru became the first prime minister of India with Sardar Vallabhbhai Patel as his deputy prime minister. The leaders of the two nations, having finally won their arduous, long-drawn struggle for freedom, now set about building their nations.

PARTITION AND INDEPENDENCE

Communal Catastrophe

India and Pakistan gained freedom in August 1947 but not peace. The newly independent nations had to pay a huge and bloody price for their partition by the British. Millions of refugees emerged from the division, fear driving them to leave their once secure homes and change countries overnight. The crossover of Hindus and Sikhs from Pakistan and Muslims from India was unprecedented in its scale and proportion. It resulted in hate, violence, bitterness and horrifying bloodbaths as Indians and Pakistanis attacked innocent men, women and children who had become refugees. An estimated one million people lost their lives in the communal hate and frenzy on both sides of the border.

The peace-loving Gandhi, then almost 78 years old, was shattered by the human catastrophe induced by the partition. The shocked and saddened Father of the Nation went on a fast unto death as a reaction against what he believed was the destruction of the country and the severance of Hindu-Muslim relations. His threat calmed the communal fever, but his drive for Hindu-Muslim unity was looked upon with suspicion by many Hindus who nicknamed him 'Mohammed Gandhi' and accused him of supporting Muslims. On 30 January 1948, less than six months after the partition, Gandhi was assassinated by a Hindu fanatic, Nathuram Godse, who resented his concern for Muslims.

Hindu Militancy

Gandhi's horrific killing during a prayer meeting brought to the fore the threat posed by Hindu nationalism. A force to reckon with in Indian politics, Hindu nationalism began to take shape in 1915 with the founding of the

Hindu Mahasabha, a loose alliance of Hindus working for cow protection, the promotion of Hindi and the rights of Hindus. Ten years later, in 1925, the Rashtriya Swayamsevak Sangh or RSS emerged and brought with it greater militancy in the drive for Hindu nationalism.

The RSS had a vision of India as a land of Hindus, for Hindus. The disciplined, cadre-based party was made up of upper class Maharashtrians, but as it grew, it drew support from people from all walks of life. Gandhi's killer, Godse, was an RSS supporter who was strongly influenced by the preaching of V D Savarkar, the most strident of the Hindu nationalists and a leader of the Hindu Mahasabha. The RSS was outlawed after Gandhi's assassination.

Kashmir

Two months after Partition, a crisis caused by armed tribal infiltrators broke out in Kashmir, which shared a border with both India and Pakistan and had acceded to neither. Maharaja Hari Singh, the prince who ruled Kashmir, turned to India for help. It was granted in return for Kashmir's accession, and India and Pakistan fought their first war over Kashmir. Even though Kashmir acceded to India, Pakistan took control of about a third of the territory. Thousands of Hindu refugees fled Kashmir for India during the fighting which stopped only after the United Nations negotiated a ceasefire. The two countries agreed to let Kashmiris vote for their future, but they have not been able to agree on how to proceed.

Kashmir, which became the state of Jammu and Kashmir when it acceded to India, has remained a source of tension for India since those early days. Both Indian and Pakistani leaders tried to reach a diplomatic agreement on the issue in the early years, but when that failed, they went to war again in 1965. The five week-long war ended in a United Nations-mandated ceasefire. At a peace conference organised by Russian Prime Minister Alexei Kosygin after the war, both sides gave their word that they would use peaceful means to solve their territorial dispute. India and Pakistan went to war for a third time in December 1971—this time over the liberation of East Pakistan. Pakistan's defeat led to the formation of the independent nation of Bangladesh.

On the Kashmir front, border skirmishes between Pakistani and Indian troops have continued over the years despite ongoing diplomatic talks. The problem has been exacerbated by Islamic terrorists seeking to weaken India's hold on the region. The skirmishes flared up in May 1999, resulting in the Kargil War, named after the icy region of Kargil in Kashmir, where the conflict took place.

India Becomes A Republic

India severed all ties with the British on 26 January 1950, the day it became an independent republic and its first president replaced the British monarch as head of state. At a solemn ceremony held in Delhi, the 34th and last governor general of India, Chakravarti Rajagopalachari, read out a proclamation announcing the birth of the Republic of India. Dr Rajendra Prasad, who was actively involved in the freedom struggle, then took the oath of office as the first president. Unlike the turmoil of the post-independence days, this time, the crowds were jubilant, holding peaceful celebrations to welcome the birth of the republic. India's new constitution was ratified on this day.

The constitution was drafted by Jawaharlal Nehru, Vallabhbhai Patel and Dr B.R. Ambedkar and was based on the 1935 Government of India Act. The constitution put in place a British style of government with two houses of parliament and the prime minister as head of government. Its federal structure allocated greater power to the central government in Delhi than the states. Kashmir was given a special autonomous status.

Politics and Policies

The Indian government, faced with the daunting task of rebuilding a poor, backward, multilingual nation with diverse religions, adopted a pragmatic policy of pluralism and secularism regarding language and religion. It tried to achieve compromise on most issues, particularly on the sensitive subject of an official language. There was widespread debate over whether Hindi or English should be adopted as the official language. Finally, in 1966, a new language law was passed, ratifying the use of both in parliament and in official dealings.

Since those early days, English has become an associate official language and the main language of business and the corporate sector, bureaucracy, and tertiary education in the country; Hindi remains the official language. Back in 1956, however, with discontent among the state governments over linguistic issues, boundaries for the states were redrawn according to language where necessary. In the south, the old Madras state was divided into Madras for those speaking Tamil, and Andhra Pradesh for the Telugu-speaking. Punjab was also split into Punjab for the Punjabi-speaking and Haryana, where the people spoke Hindi. Bengal became the state of West Bengal. Many cities have been renamed after India's independence. These include Bombay, changed to Mumbai, Calcutta to Kolkata and Madras to Chennai.

Democratic India held parliamentary and state elections in 1952, 1957 and 1962, and the Congress Party won majorities in the Lok Sabha (Lower House) and the state legislatures every time. With these electoral victories, the Congress increased its support reaching out to the grassroots level and religious minorities, particularly Muslims. The Congress faced opposition from the Communists, the Socialists and the right-wing Swatantra Party and the Jan Sangh, but these groups were largely fragmented, which helped the Congress Party increase its power and influence.

The Nehru Legacy

The Nehru family has played an important role in Indian politics from the days of Motilal Nehru, a wealthy Anglicised lawyer who played a significant role in Mahatma Gandhi's freedom movement during British rule, and in the Congress Party. But it was his son Jawaharlal who took the Nehru name to the pinnacle of Indian politics when he became the first prime minister of free India on 15 August 1947. Jawaharlal was succeeded by his daughter Indira Gandhi as Congress Party leader and prime minister, and subsequently by his grandson, Rajiv Gandhi. The Nehru family's leadership of the Congress Party since India's independence has led to accusations of dynastic rule.

Like his father, Jawaharlal played an active part in India's freedom struggle and in the Congress Party, and was a keen supporter of Mahatma Gandhi, who had nominated him as his political heir. Jawaharlal was educated at

Harrow and Cambridge in Britain and later followed his father into the law profession. His role in negotiating independence with the British won him the position of India's first prime minister. Influenced by the Soviet style of economic planning, Jawaharlal launched a socialist experiment in democratic India as opposed to the capitalism prevalent in the United States and other Western countries. Central planning was the key feature of his economic policy, with five-year plans guiding India's growth in agriculture, industry and other areas of the economy. He also set India on the path of non-alignment in foreign relations and made it a key member of the Non-Aligned Movement. Jawaharlal was one of the five founders of the movement, which held its first summit in Belgrade, Yugoslavia, in September 1961. He believed that by staying neutral, India could concentrate on development rather than defence.

From a poor, backward country, depleted by plundering, exploitation and colonisation at the time of independence in 1947, India has become a world power today due to its strong democratic foundation and the hard work, intellectual capability, creativity and entrepreneurial spirit of its people. India's leaders have made mistakes along the way, but the Indian people have assiduously kept the country on track, taking it to ever greater heights of growth and progress.

RELIGION

Religion is an integral part of life in India, a spiritually diverse nation that is the birthplace of two of the great faiths of the world, Hinduism and Buddhism. These two faiths, along with Jainism, Sikhism, Islam, Christianity and Zoroastrianism, comprise the main religions of secular India. Many of these faiths share common concepts such as a belief in karma and reincarnation. The law of *karma* states that a person's deeds, both good and bad, determine all his experiences, thus making him entirely responsible for his own life. While religious strife is rampant in the country, particularly between Hindus and Muslims, India is committed to secularism as laid down in its constitution. The majority of its people remain staunch supporters of communal harmony and peaceful co-existence of all religions.

HINDUISM

Hinduism is the third largest religion in the world by devotees and the predominant religion of India, practised by around 80.5 per cent of the country's population, or almost 828 million of its people (2001 census). It doesn't have a single founder nor a single holy book but a number of sacred texts, namely the *Vedas*, *Upanishads*, *Puranas*, the *Bhagavad Gita* and the epic poems of the *Mahabharata* and the *Ramayana*, which provide spiritual and practical guidance.

Hinduism originated 3,000 years ago during India's ancient Indus Valley Civilisation (2800 BC–1900 BC). It has many different tenets and practices, centred around Brahman, the supreme cosmic who is worshipped in many forms. Brahman is an eternal soul who is present in everything, and is represented by a triumvirate of gods consisting of Brahma the Creator, Vishnu the Preserver and Shiva the Destroyer and Re-creator. Lakshmi, the consort of Vishnu, is the goddess of wealth, knowledge and purity and a popular deity in the Hindu pantheon, which also includes Rama, Hanuman and Krishna, each embodying different attributes of Brahman.

Hindus believe in idol worship and many of the devout have a shrine at home with images of their favourite gods to whom they devote daily prayers and offerings of flowers, incense, fruit or even money. Devotees visit temples weekly or during special occasions and festivals where, besides making offerings to the gods, they hear priests recite from the holy scriptures.

Pilgrimages are an important part of Hinduism, and Hindus travel to sacred Hindu sites such as Vaishno Devi in the north or Tirupati in the south of the country, to seek divine blessings and to see and be seen by the deity. The city of Varanasi, situated on the banks of the Ganges River, is also a favourite pilgrimage spot. The Ganges is revered as holy by Hindus and worshipped as Goddess Ganga. It is believed that bathing in the Ganges will cleanse one of one's sins, and ritual bathing is performed once in 12 years at the Kumbh Mela Festival in the northern city of Allahabad, at the confluence of the Ganges and Yamuna rivers.

The *Vedas* (*Books of Knowledge*) are ancient texts introduced to India during the Vedic Civilisation in the middle of the second millennium b.c. These ancient texts in Sanskrit define the meaning of Hinduism for Hindus. The *Bhagavad Gita* or *Song of the Lord* is another important Hindu text that preaches loyalty to God and extols the benefits of duty, knowledge, work and devotion, which are paths to salvation. It is contained in the sixth book of the *Mahabharata*, the Hindu epic which has the distinction of being the world's longest poem. The other Hindu epic, the *Ramayana*, was composed in the same period and tells the story of Prince Rama, an incarnation of Hindu god Vishnu.

Sacrifice was the most significant rite of the Vedic tradition and was used to invoke the gods, notably the warrior gods Varuna and Indra who represented good over the powers of evil. The rituals were performed by

Brahmin priests, but by 500 BC, with the growth of cities and the emergence of the merchant class, the old order of Hindu Brahmin priests faced a challenge from their followers, who questioned their monopoly and who turned to teachers such as Siddhartha Gautama who achieved enlightenment to become the Buddha.

FOOD FOR THE GODS

Special dishes are prepared for the Hindu gods on their celebration days held at temples. Ganesh, the Elephant God, is believed to have a taste for sweet dumplings made of rice flour while the southern savoury *vadai* is prepared for Hanuman, the Monkey God. Krishna, on the other hand, has a preference for milk products. According to legend, he helped himself to buttermilk and yoghurt from the kitchen as a young boy when his mother wasn't looking. The food is prepared in the temple kitchens and then distributed to devotees who come to worship.

It was at this time that Hindu sages began preaching the search for Brahman in the soul of all humans through ascetism, meditation and yoga. Their growing concern was to achieve release (*moksha*) from the material world and from the cycle of birth, death and rebirth (*samsara*) and the concept of *karma* grew in importance. Both the principles of *karma* and *samsara* are contained in the *Upanishads*.

Hindu philosophy evolved from the 4th to the 12th centuries, based on the sacred texts of the *Puranas*, which introduced the triumvirate of Brahma, Vishnu and Shiva into Hinduism. The *Puranas*, written in a simple language, also elaborated on sacred rites, pilgrimages, caste relations and how to portray divine images.

As Hinduism evolved, gods such as Ganesha, Krishna and Hanuman gained in importance and developed a huge following. The various gods of the Hindu pantheon have different attributes and powers but are all visible representations of Brahman. They are believed to answer prayers, fight evil or provide guidance within the real world. The Hindu pantheon exists in its full glory today, with each region of the country embracing its own particular deities. In the southern states of Tamil Nadu and Kerala, for instance, Ayyappan and Murugan are the incarnations of Shiva and are worshipped as protectors of the village. Rites and rituals also vary from region to region with a plethora of temples, priests, gurus and other spiritual teachers propagating everything from yoga to meditation, self-denial, contemplation and detachment as a way to seek the truth and liberate the soul from worldly desire.

OM

'Om' is the most sacred of sounds in Hinduism and is said to be the syllable that preceded the universe. According to Hindu mythology, the gods were made from 'Om', which is a cosmic vibration that holds the heavens together. Because of its sacred nature, 'Om' precedes all Hindu prayer and is also used as the final exclamation, similar to 'Amen' in Christianity.

BUDDHISM

Buddhism, which originated 2,500 years ago, was born in India at a time when the idea of reincarnation—the constant cycle of birth, death and rebirth—was growing among Hindus. Buddhism focuses on personal spiritual development and strives for an insight into the truths of life. Its founder is Siddhartha Gautama, a young prince who advocated purity and goodness as a way to escape the cycle of reincarnation.

Siddhartha, the son of King Shuddhodana and his queen Maya, was born in 563 BC at Lumbini, near Kapilavastu, capital of the Sakyan republic, a region that lies in present-day southern Nepal. The young Siddhartha was disenchanted with his life of luxury and was particularly traumatised when he went into the city and saw sickness, death and suffering among the people. He realised that all living beings had to experience the sufferings of birth, sickness, ageing and death, and that the suffering was repeated in each rebirth. He developed a desire to release mankind from this suffering and, at the age of 29, left the palace and his family and became an ascetic, renouncing all worldly pleasures. At the age of 35, Siddhartha reached Bodh Gaya in the northern Indian state of Bihar. Here he attained enlightenment or *nirvana*, a state of blissful peace devoid of all desire, while meditating beneath a *bodhi* tree. He became Buddha, the Awakened One.

For the next 45 years until his death, the Buddha travelled across the country, teaching the Wheels of Dharma which includes the Four Noble Truths and the Noble Eightfold Path. The Four Noble Truths are: suffering is the condition of all existence; suffering is due to desire, craving and selfishness; suffering can be overcome; and the way to overcome it is by following the Eightfold Path, which leads to right viewpoint, values, speech, actions, livelihood, effort, mindfulness and meditation. The Buddha preached the doctrine of *anatta* (non-self), refuting the existence of a permanent self, which he believed was the cause of most of human suffering. He also preached the Middle Way or Middle Path, which is the practice of moderation, as opposed to the extremes of self-indulgence and self-mortification. His medium of communication was believed to be Magadhi, the language of Magadha.

Buddhism has two main sects, Theravada and Mahayana, though many more have evolved over the generations, with each sect establishing many different schools. Mahayana Buddhism came into being at the end of the first millennium BC, and is widely practised in countries such as China, Tibet, Japan and Korea. The Theravada sect stresses the importance of monastic life and austerity and believes in Siddhartha Gautama as the only Buddha; the Mahayana sect emphasises that enlightenment is open to anyone who follows the path of devotion and sees Siddhartha Gautama as one of many Buddhas.

During the reign of Mauryan Emperor Ashoka (272 BC–231 BC) the Buddha's philosophy acquired a national status. Ashoka converted to Buddhism and tried to bring about a moral and spiritual revival in his kingdom. He is also credited with helping spread Buddhism beyond India; however, by the 4th and 5th centuries, Buddhism was in decline in India while gaining popularity in Central Asia and China. It witnessed a revival under the Guptas (320–550) but declined when royal patronage was withdrawn in subsequent years, and stupas and monasteries were destroyed. The rise of Hinduism was another reason for the lack of patronage of Buddhism.

In present-day India, Buddhism is practised by about 7.9 million people or 0.8 per cent of the population (2001 census).

JAINISM

Jainism is the most ascetically demanding of all Indian religions. It preaches that the way to liberation from the cycle of rebirth is to live a life of renunciation. It also advocates refrain from doing harm to any living thing, a concept known as *ahimsa*. Jainism does not have one main god but has several lesser deities for different aspects of life.

Modern Jainism was founded by Vardhamana, called Mahavira, a contemporary of the Buddha in the 6th century BC. Both Mahavira and the Buddha were of noble birth and renounced all worldly possessions to live the life of ascetics at about the same time.

The three guiding principles of Jainism, known as the Three Jewels, are: right belief, right knowledge and right conduct. All devotees must abide by the five *mahavratas* (five great vows): non-violence, non-attachment to possessions, not lying, not stealing and sexual restraint. Jains are strict vegetarians and are required to carry out some spiritual act every day. They are divided into two major sects: the Digambara (Sky Clad) and the Svetambara (White Clad). The Svetambara Jain sect conducts a ceremony known as the eightfold *puja*, during which the worshipper makes eight symbolic offerings to the image of a *tirthankara* (historical teacher).

Mahavira had 11 disciples, each entrusted with a band of about 300 to 500 monks to preach the religion. Bhadrabahu, contemporary of the great Mauryan King Chandragupta Maurya (r.321 BC–297 BC), was the greatest propagator of the faith after Mahavira. After Bhadrabahu's death, serious differences began to arise in the Jain community. The group led by Bhadrabahu migrated towards the west coast and Deccan, while others remained in the north. The texts containing the teachings of Mahavira are called the *Agamas* and form the canonical literature of Svetambara Jainism. Mahavira's disciples compiled his words into texts or sutras and memorised them to pass on to future generations. Jain monks and nuns were not allowed to possess religious books as part of their vow of non-acquisition, nor were they allowed to write. As centuries passed, some of the texts were forgotten or distorted. Many Jain monks died during a famine around 350 BC, and with them, the memory of many Jain texts died too.

It was in the Gupta period (320–550) that Gujarat became the most important centre of Jainism in India. The great council of the religion, which saw the holy scriptures finally put into writing, was held at Valabhi in the state of Gujarat around 460. By the Gupta period, Jainism was also well established in other parts of the country, including Rajasthan.

In spite of its relatively small size, the Jain community, whose members are mostly from the mercantile class, has had a strong influence on Indian life. There are splendid examples of Jain temples and sculptures of their *tirthankaras* in different parts of the country. The best of Jain temple architecture, however, is to be found at Ginar, Palitana and Mount Abu in Rajasthan. Jains have also made valuable contributions in literature and painting.

During the 20th century, Jainism was carried beyond India with the migration of some of its followers from western India to eastern Africa, particularly Kenya and Uganda. Political unrest in these countries in the 1960s forced many Jains to relocate to Britain, where the first Jain temple outside India was consecrated in Leicester. Jains subsequently moved to the United States and Canada, where they successfully assumed their traditional mercantile occupations.

NOT ALLOWED TO HARM INSECTS

The principle of non-violence affects every aspect of the daily life of Jains, from walking barefoot in case a living thing is harmed underfoot, to preparing food in such a way as to ensure that no living form is eaten in the process. They do not eat after dark to avoid accidentally consuming insects, and ascetics are required to wear masks to avoid inhaling living organisms in the air.

ISLAM

Islam, the second largest religion in the world, has as many as 138.2 million followers in India or 13.4 per cent of the population (2001 census). This makes India the country with the second largest Muslim population after Indonesia. Muslims believe in one god, Allah, and base their laws on their holy book, the Qur'an, and the Sunnah, the practical principles of their religious leader Prophet Muhammad. The most important Muslim practices are the five basic Pillars of Islam: the declaration of faith, praying five times a day, giving money to charity, fasting and a once-in-a-lifetime pilgrimage to Mecca.

Muslims believe that Islam has always existed, but that the final revelation of their religion was made through Prophet Muhammad in the 7th century in the holy city of Mecca. In subsequent centuries, Islam spread across the Middle East and Asia through Muslim communities, traders or through conquest. According to historical records, it was brought to India in the 7th century by Arab merchants who propagated the religion wherever they went. In subsequent years, the spread of Islam was consolidated through Muslim invaders.

Full-scale Muslim conquests of India began in the 10th to 11th centuries headed by Mahmud of Ghazni, which further consolidated the spread of Islam in the country. The Khilji, Tughlaq, Sayyid and Lodhi dynasties of the Delhi Sultanate, as well as the Mughal Empire in the 16th to 18th centuries contributed to the fusion of Hindu and Islamic thought, art and architecture and the development of the Persian and Urdu languages.

The centuries of Islamic rulers saw the rapid spread of Islam through India, both through peaceful means and forcible conversions. Islamic mystics known as Sufis played a key role in the spread of Islam in India. They succeeded in propagating the tenets of Islam in an unorthodox way which appealed to Hindus. Moreover, under the Mughals, Hindus were subjected to harsh taxation—the hated Islamic poll tax or *jizya* and another pilgrimage tax, which forced many Hindus to convert to Islam. Mughal Emperor Akbar, the most benevolent of the Mughal rulers, abolished the pilgrimage tax in 1563 and the *jizya* poll tax the following year, but the *jizya* was reinstated by Mughal Emperor Aurangzeb in 1679. The Masjid-i-Jahan Numan, better known as the Jama Masjid, is the largest and most prominent mosque in India. It was built by Mughal Emperor Shah Jahan and is located in the old part of Delhi.

Today, the Muslims of India, like the rest of the Muslim world, are divided into two main sects, Sunni and Shia. There are also many different sub-sects. In west India are to be found the Bohra and Khoja communities;

in the state of Kerala in south India exists the Mophilla community; while in the north are the Pathans.

CHRISTIANITY

Christianity first came to India in the year 52, with the arrival of St Thomas, an apostle of Jesus Christ, in the southern Indian state of Kerala. St Thomas converted the local people to the Christian way of life, but it was not until the arrival of Portuguese missionaries such as St Francis Xavier and missionaries from Spain, Germany, Italy and France in the 15th century that Christianity was firmly established in the country.

The Portuguese Roman Catholics, led by St Francis Xavier, moved westward towards Goa, where they sought to convert the entire Hindu population. During the Goa inquisition under the Portuguese, Hindus were forced to convert and those who refused or were suspected of practising heresy were burnt alive in public. In the early 18th century, Protestant missionaries became active in the country, leading to the establishment of different Christian communities. The missionaries set up schools, churches, charitable organisations for the poor and destitute and even acquired proficiency in the local languages. Some of them, such as Italian Jesuit Constant Joseph Beschi who composed the Tamil epic, *Thembavani*, even contributed to the great body of Indian literature. The Bible was translated into different Indian languages by missionaries.

There are 24 million Christians in India today or 2.3 per cent of the population (2001 census). The majority of Christians can be found in Goa as well as Nagaland, Mizoram, Manipur and Meghalaya in the north-east and the southern states of Tamil Nadu and Kerala. In the rest of India, they are present in smaller numbers across a wide stretch from Kolkata in Bengal, Bihar, Uttar Pradesh, Madhya Pradesh to Mumbai-Pune in Maharashtra.

Popular Christian pilgrimage sites include: St Thomas Cathedral at Mylapore in Chennai where the grave of Apostle St Thomas is venerated; St Xavier's shrine at Bom Jesus Church in old Goa; the Church of Our Lady of the Mount at Bandra, in Mumbai; the Church of Our Lady of Health at Vailankanni in Tamil Nadu; and the Shrine of St Theresa of Avila at Mahe, close to Tellicherry in north Kerala.

MOTHER TERESA

Mother Teresa came to Kolkata as a missionary in 1931, but for Agnes Gonxha Bojaxhiu (the name she was born with in Albania), her calling lay outside the walls of the St Mary's convent school where she taught. In 1948, she started an open air school for slum children and later established her own order, the Missionaries of Charity, to care for the discarded of Kolkata society. Since then the Missionaries of Charity has spread throughout the world and Mother Teresa has been highly acclaimed for her outstanding work with the poor. She was awarded the Nobel Peace Prize in 1979 and in October 2003 was beatified by Pope John Paul II. She died on 5 September 1997.

SIKHISM

Sikhism was born in the northern Indian state of Punjab in the 16th century. It was founded by Guru Nanak, a social reformer who propagated a transcendent, formless divinity that exists everywhere. Sikhism is a monotheistic religion and it stresses carrying out good deeds, living honestly and caring for others, rather than rituals and rites. The Sikh place of worship is called a *gurdwara* and the Sikh holy book is the *Guru Granth Sahib*.

Sikhism shares the concepts of *karma* and rebirth with other Indian religious traditions such as Hinduism, Buddhism and Jainism. Sikh spirituality is centred around the need to understand and experience God, and eventually become one with God. A Sikh serves God by serving other people every day, a concept known as *seva*. By devoting their lives to service, they get rid of their own ego and pride. Many Sikhs carry out chores in the gurdwara as their service to the community; these range from working in the kitchen to cleaning the floor. The *langar*, or free food kitchen, is another community service. Sikhs are recognised by their turbans worn over long hair and their unshaven beards, both signs of their religious faith. Every Sikh also considers it an obligation to wear a *kara* (steel bangle).

Guru Nanak taught unity and reform to his followers in India, and as a mark of their devotion to him, they called themselves Sikhs, derived from the Sanskrit '*shishya*', meaning 'disciple'. Guru Angad succeeded Guru Nanak who died in 1539. Subsequent gurus who continued the teachings of Guru Nanak were Amar Das; Ram Das; Arjun, whose death by torture on the orders of Mughal Emperor Jahangir brought militancy to Sikhism; Hargobind; Har Rai; Har Krishan; Tegh Bahadur, who laid down his life for his people; and Govind Singh, the tenth and last guru who died in 1708. Govind Singh decreed that after his death, the spiritual guide of the Sikhs would be the teachings contained in the *Guru Granth Sahib*. The spiritual book has the status of a guru and is venerated as the living presence of the gurus. It is a collection of the teachings of Guru Nanak and other Sikh gurus, and is written in Gurmukhi script, which literally means 'from the mouth of the Guru'. It was Govind Singh who established the Sikh army known as the Khalsa.

Sikhs can be found in different parts of India and abroad, but they are concentrated in the state of Punjab where the Sikh holy city of Amritsar is located. The premier Sikh shrine, the Golden Temple, is built on an island in a huge sacred water tank known as the Amrita Saras (Pool of Nectar) in Amritsar.

GURU NANAK

Guru Nanak was born in 1469 to Kalyan Chand and Tripti in 'Nankana Sahib', a village in present-day Pakistan. Dismayed that Nanak did not seem inclined towards any useful vocation, his father sent him to Sultanpur where his daughter Nanaki lived with her husband. There, Nanak was put to work in a local store but instead of selling goods, he distributed them free to the poor. At the age of 27, Nanak left Sultanpur and embarked on his preaching odysseys called *udasis*. He refused to accept distinctions between people on the basis of caste or creed and taught everyone how to look beyond these barriers. Guru Nanak's attitude towards Hindus and Muslims led some to depict him as a reconciler of the two religions.

ZOROASTRIANISM

An old religion, founded in what is now Azarbaijan in the 6th century BC, Zoroastrianism teaches the duties of man according to the law of nature, which Zarathushtra, the founder of Zoroastrianism, called the law of Asha. Fire and the sun are the emblems of Zoroastrianism.

Zarathushtra is said to have been born around the 6th century BC in Azarbaijan. He spent several years in meditation, reflecting on life and human existence, until he discovered perfect power or energy and perfect wisdom. His religion was universal and advanced for an age when people were still practising a primitive form of polytheism. He preached that a better life could be achieved with the help of an invisible god of wisdom, truth, light and goodness, rather than a set of superstitious rituals. Zarathushtra emphasised doing good towards one's fellow man; hence the motto of the religion is 'Good thoughts, good words, good deeds'.

The religion's holy texts, the *Gathas*, are sacred songs written while Zarathushtra meditated on a mountain. Other scriptures were later written by his disciples in Eastern Iran. There are five *Gathas*: *Gatha Ahunavaiti*, on freedom of choice; *Gatha Ushtavaiti*, on supreme bliss (*ushta*); *Gatha Spenta Mainya*, on the holy spirit; *Gatha Vohu Kshathra*, on the good kingdom; and *Gatha Vahishtoishti*, on sovereign desire or fulfillment.

The Zoroastrian scriptures were neglected and even lost in a fire at one time in their chequered history. It was only during the reign of Ardeshir Papakan, who founded the last Zoroastrian Empire in Iran called the Sassanian Empire, that a concise prayer book called the *Khordeh Avesta* was composed. This book contains prayers and passages on astronomy and medicine.

The followers of Zoroastrianism are called Parsis, a term derived from Parsa, the name of a province in south-western Iran in ancient times. Around 766, a small group of Iranian Parsis set sail in open sailing vessels and landed at Divo Dui, a tiny island at the tip of Kathiawar, in what is now the western Indian state of Gujarat. They settled there to practise their faith and later spread along the west coast of Gujarat where they settled down as farmers, fruit growers, toddy planters, carpenters and weavers. The Parsis were excellent weavers and they have left a legacy of three ancient crafts, namely the Surti *ghat*, the *garo* and the *tanchoi*. All three are exquisite silk textiles differing in texture and design. The Surti *ghat* is a soft silk with a satin finish, while the *garo* is fine embroidered silk and the *tanchoi* is a type of rich floral brocade.

In present-day India, the Parsis are mostly found in Mumbai, the commercial capital of India. They pray at fire temples. The holiest of these temples in India is the Atash Behram at Udvada, near Mumbai, where the Sacred Fire brought by Iranian refugees from Iran has been burning continuously since 1741.

PEOPLE AND
LANGUAGES

POPULATION

India is a country of diversity and contrasts. The seventh largest in the world, it is a vast land spread across 3,287,263 sq km. Its diversity is evident in its physical features, with the majestic Himalayan mountain range in the north, tropical rain forests in the south, and the Gangetic Plain and the Thar Desert region in between. India is a sovereign socialist seculardemocratic republic with a parliamentary system of government. It is divided into 28 states, six union territories and one national capital territory of Delhi.

India has a remarkable multiethnic and multilingual population, developed from its long and chequered history of invasions and migrations from the West, the Middle East, Central Asia, China and Tibet. With 1.028 billion people (2001 census) it is the second most populated country and accounts for 16.7 per cent of the world's population. About 72 per cent of the people live in the country's 593,643 villages; the rest live in urban centres.

The major ethnic groups are Indo-Aryan (72 per cent), Dravidian (25 per cent), Mongoloid and others (3 per cent). The Indo-Aryans are descendants of the Indic branch of the ancient Indo-Iranians (also known as Aryans) and are mainly found in the northern and central parts of India. The Dravidians, who arrived in India before the Aryans, are concentrated in the south, and the Mongoloids in the north-east. The Mongoloids can also be found in the state of West Bengal and the Ladakh region of Jammu and Kashmir.

CASTE AND RESERVATION

Caste—a division of people into a hierarchy of communities—is believed to have been started by the Aryans in order to achieve a social order in ancient India. This caste system comprised four broad categories—Brahmin, Kshatriya, Vaishya, Shudra. While modern Indian society does not adhere to the caste system, discrimination over caste still exists and can sometimes lead to clashes and community tension. To protect the welfare of the underprivileged members of society, whom the government calls the 'backward classes' or 'scheduled castes', the Indian government has set up a special division in the Ministry of Welfare to look after their needs. It has also adopted a policy of positive discrimination towards these people, as well as towards the aboriginal tribals it calls the 'scheduled tribes'. A reservation policy, whereby a small percentage of seats are reserved for these underprivileged in educational institutions and government jobs, has led to resentment and protests from the rest of Indian society.

OFFICIAL LANGUAGES

India has 22 officially recognised languages as laid down by the constitution. Of these, Hindi is the official language of the federal government in Delhi and the language spoken by the largest percentage of the people. The other 21 languages are Assamese, Bengali, Bodo, Dogri, Gujarati, Kannada, Kashmiri, Konkani, Maithili, Malayalam, Manipuri, Marathi, Nepali, Oriya, Punjabi, Sanskrit, Santhali, Sindhi, Tamil, Telugu and Urdu. English is an associate official language. Most of the languages spoken in the north and centre are of Aryan origin, the ones prevalent in the south are Dravidian, and Sini-Mongoloid languages dominate in the east of India. Tamil is one of the major Dravidian languages, and the oldest, with a long literary tradition dating back to 500 BC when the first Tamil literature, *Sangam*, was created.

Besides the official languages, there are also hundreds of minor languages and dialects spoken in the country, which come from either the Austro-Asiatic or the Tibeto-Burman linguistic families. Then there are the Andamanese languages, spoken on the Andaman Islands, which are not linked to any of the other families. Dialects are referred to as mother tongues and may be spoken by millions even though they are not recognised by the government.

After independence in 1947, India was divided into different states with the boundaries created on linguistic and religious lines. Each state has its own principal language, or in some cases, two or even three, that are used by its people. A good example of this is the north-eastern state of Sikkim which lists Lepcha, Bhutia and Nepali as its main languages. The Andaman and Nicobar Islands, a union territory in the Bay of Bengal, has as many as six principal languages—Hindi, Nicobarese, Bengali, Tamil, Malayalam and Telugu. In the case of Sikkim, while Lepcha and Bhutia are listed as principal languages, they are not recognised by the government. Neither is Nicobarese, spoken in Andaman and Nicobar.

DRAVIDIAN LANGUAGES

The Dravidian languages are believed to have derived from an ancient language spoken in India before the advent of the Aryans in 1500 BC. There are four major Dravidian languages: Kannada, Malayalam, Tamil and Telugu, each of which has millions of speakers spread across southern India. In the Dravidian languages, verbs have a negative and an affirmative voice. The languages also make extensive use of suffixes with nouns and verbs. They have their own script, which is related to the Devanagri script used for Hindi. A prominent feature of the Dravidian languages is the way the sounds are created at the front of the mouth.

SANSKRIT

Sanskrit occupies a central place in Indian history, being the language of the *Vedas*, the ancient Indian scriptures that laid the foundation of Hinduism in the country. Belonging to the Indic group of the Indo-European family of languages, Sanskrit first surfaced in India during the Vedic period (1700 BC–500 BC) in the *Rig Veda*, the oldest Vedic scripture. It evolved into classical Sanskrit when it was used as a standard court language in 400 BC. It was also used for religious and learned discourses by the upper classes and nobles and became the medium of Hindu literature. It was the grammarian Panini who in 500 BC wrote about Sanskrit grammar in the *Astadhyayi* (Eight-Chapter Grammar), which was essentially a treatise which defined correct Sanskrit—its nouns, pronouns, verbs, adjectives and three genders. Sanskrit was written in the

Brahmi and Kharosthi alphabets, though the Devanagri script, descended from Brahmi, is also used to write Sanskrit.

Classical Sanskrit gradually gave way to the vernacular dialects, known as Prakrits, which in turn evolved into the modern languages of Hindi, Gujarati, Bengali, Tamil, Telugu and Kannada, among others. Today, Sanskrit is mostly used during religious Hindu rituals.

THE PRAKRITS AND PALI

The Prakrits (Sanskrit for 'natural') are vernacular dialects of classical Sanskrit (meaning 'perfected'), which came into use by the 6th century BC. They were grammatically simpler than Sanskrit, hence their popularity among the masses. The higher status of Sanskrit compared to Prakrit was apparent in Sanskrit dramas, where Sanskrit was spoken by upper class characters, while Prakrit was spoken by lower class characters. Pali, the language of the Buddhists and their sacred literature, is a Prakrit. So is Magadhi, the language of the Magadha Kingdom. Later Indian languages such as Hindi, Punjabi and Bengali are believed to have descended from the Prakrits. The dialects are classified under Middle Indic languages, while Sanskrit is considered Old Indic.

HINDI

Hindi is a direct descendant of Sanskrit through Prakrit. Its development has also been influenced by non-Indian languages such as Turkish, Persian, Arabic and Portuguese. Hindi's present form is derived from Hindustani, a colloquial form of the language which was spoken in north India in the 9th and 10th centuries. It was given the name Hindvi, the language of Hind (the land of the Indus River), by the Persian-speaking Turks during the days of the Delhi Sultanate (11th–13th centuries). Hindvi was made up of Sanskrit, Arabic and Persian words and developed into a mixed language of communication between the locals and the new arrivals. The government settled on Hindvi, among the different dialects in use in the Sultanate, as the language of communication. The language travelled to other parts as the Sultanate grew and became a literary language in the 18th century. It finally split into Hindi and Urdu, with Hindi acquiring the status of a national language during British colonial rule.

Hindi is written in the Devanagri script and has 57 symbols, including 10 vowels and 40 consonants. Vowels are combined with consonants and appear in the form of a line or mark known as a *matra* above, below, after or before the consonant. The script has no capital letters and is written from left to right horizontally. It includes honorifics which allow adjustments in communication in formal and informal conversations. Devanagri is straightforward and easy to learn with the words written according to the way they are spoken. Hindi shares common features with Urdu, the official language of Jammu and Kashmir state, and Pakistan, as well as other Indian languages such as Bengali, Punjabi and Gujarati.

BRAHMI SCRIPT

Brahmi is the earliest known script used for writing Sanskrit. It originated in the 5th century BC and was used by Maurya Emperor Ashoka (r. 273 BC–232 BC), to inscribe his famous edicts on stones and pillars in the kingdom. Brahmi is a 'syllabic alphabet', which means that each character is made up of a consonant as well as a neutral vowel. In Brahmi, the same consonant is used with extra strokes in combination with different vowels.

PEOPLE AND LANGUAGES

LITERATURE

Indian literary works are as diverse as the languages spoken in the country and include everything from epics, lyrics, poetry, aphorisms, drama, fables, folk stories to scientific prose. Traditional literature is dominated by religious themes from Hinduism, with writers singing praises of the gods and invoking their blessings. The entire corpus of Vedic texts—the *Puranas*, the epics the *Ramayana* and the *Mahabharata*, the *Bhagavad Gita*—and renowned poet Kalidas' *Abhijnana Shakuntala* are some of the celebrated works from this genre. The *Puranas*, 18 in number, are ancient Sanskrit texts that are said to pre-date the epics. The *Puranas* discuss the creation of the universe, the powers of the gods and the genealogies of kings.

Most of early Indian literature was in the Sanskrit language, the dominant language of intellectual pursuits at that time; however, in south India during ancient times, literary works were written in the Tamil language. During the period of Muslim rule from the 11th century onwards, classical Persian poetry took centre stage, giving way to Urdu literature during the Mughal period. By the 16th century, an exhaustive written literature in the vernacular languages had appeared. In the early 19th century, prose in different Indian languages got an impetus with the setting up of vernacular schools, with Bengali writers taking the lead. The British brought English literature to India, and it had a profound influence on many writers of that period who assimilated some of its elements to Indian themes.

Today there is an extensive body of literature in all the important languages of India, as well as an impressive collection of works in English. Illustrious Indian writers of the 19th and early 20th centuries include Ram Mohun Roy, Bankim Chandra Chatterjee, Prem Chand, a renowned writer known as the Father of Urdu short stories, Vivekananda and Nobel laureate Rabindranath Tagore, who won the 1913 Nobel Prize in Literature. Tulsidas, who lived in the 17th century, is considered the greatest Hindi poet, while Mirza Asadullah Baig Khan, or Ghalib, was the greatest Urdu poet of the 19th century. Muhammad Iqbal was a celebrated Muslim poet of the 20th century.

Among the later writers are Nirad C Chaudhuri, R K Narayan, Salman Rushdie, Rohinton Mistry, Vikram Chandra, Vikram Seth, Anita Desai, Jhumpa Lahiri, Arundhati Roy and Kiran Desai, many of whom represent the new breed of Indians writing in English for a national as well as an international audience. Salman Rushdie, Arundhati Roy and Kiran Desai have been honoured by the international community with the prestigious Booker Prize, while Jhumpa Lahiri has received the Pulitzer Prize for fiction for her debut collection of short stories.

It was Salman Rushdie's 1981 novel *Midnight's Children* that set the trend of Indian authors writing in English. This trend has seen a newfound resurgence in recent years. The number of Indians writing in English has mushroomed in the 21st century with more and more writers, particularly those belonging to the diaspora in the United States and Canada, drawing on their personal experiences in post-colonial India or their lives overseas, to spin a fascinating story centred around their unique identity.

AUTOBIOGRAPHY OF AN UNKNOWN INDIAN

Nirad C Chaudhuri is best known for his *Autobiography of an Unknown Indian*, a controversial book about his experiences as a Bengali under British rule. The book is rated as Chaudhuri's magnum opus for his vivid articulation of middle class Bengali society in the early 1900s. Chaudhuri, an eccentric Anglophile who offended many Indians because of his open admiration for the British Raj, moved to Britain in the 1970s and lived in Oxford until his death in August 1999 at the age of 101. He continued to write while at Oxford, penning his last book, an anti-India, pro-British collection of essays titled *Three Horsemen of the New Apocalypse*, when he was 99.

TRADITIONAL LITERATURE

The Vedas

The *Vedas* (the word literally means 'knowledge') are the primary source of information about the ancient Vedic period (1700 BC– 500 BC) in Indian history, and are believed to have been composed by 1200 BC–800 BC. The lyrical texts were passed on orally from generation to generation through memorisation and recitation until the time when they were written down. They contain hymns in praise of Aryan gods such as Indra, Surya, Agni and Varuna; rituals, spells, charms and magic formulae to guide priests; and general philosophical teachings. The main ritual referred to in the texts is sacrifice, which was at the core of Aryan religion. The *Vedas* also carry information on mathematics, science, traditional systems of medicine and yoga.

The *Samhitas* are the most ancient of the *Vedas* and consist of the *Rig-Veda*, *Yajur-Veda*, *Sama-Veda* and *Atharva-Veda*. The *Samhitas* are followed by the *Brahmanas*, *Aranyakas* and the *Upanishads*.

The oldest and most significant text of the entire body of Vedic literature is the *Rig-Veda* (*Hymns of Praise*). It is a collection of 1,028 hymns spread over 10 books, the earliest originating in c.1200 BC. According to legend, the hymns of the *Rig-Veda* were delivered by Brahman himself to Aryan priests who then passed it down through the generations. One of the first hymns praises Agni, the God of Fire, while another hymn talks about the process of creation.

The *Sama-Veda*, *Yajur-Veda* and the *Atharva-Veda* came after the *Rig-Veda* and dealt with chanting, rituals and sacrifices, and magical incantations respectively. The *Brahmanas* gave extensive details of prayer and rituals and specified practices to be carried out by the wealthy and the elite members of society. The *Aranyakas* are forest texts, with knowledge that can only be learned in the secluded environment of forests. The *Upanishads* were taught to those who sat down beside their teachers, *upa* meaning 'near', *ni* meaning 'down' and *shad* meaning 'sit', hence their name. Composed between 800 BC and 200 BC, they are believed to have reshaped Hindu belief by instilling philosophical knowledge into Hinduism. They contain 200 works in prose and verse, and deal with religion, philosophy and the creation of the universe.

RAMAYANA

Of the two Hindu epics, the *Ramayana* is older. It is believed to have been composed in 1500 BC, although it was only written down in Sanskrit by the sage Valmiki in 400 BC. It is one of the pivotal literary works of ancient India with two important Indian festivals, Dussehra and Diwali, emanating from it. The *Ramayana* is divided into seven sections and explores the values of valour, devotion, duty and morality through the story of Prince Rama, the seventh incarnation of the Hindu god Vishnu.

According to the story, Rama is the eldest son of King Dasaratha, who rules the kingdom of Kosala in Ayodhya. The king has three wives, one of whom, Kaikeyi, saves his life after he is injured in battle. As a reward for her efforts, the devious Kaikeyi asks that her son Bharatha be crowned king while the rightful heir, Rama, be banished from the kingdom for 14 years. The principled and uprighteous Rama goes into exile with his wife Sita and brother, Lakshmana, turning down the pleas of Bharatha, who is next in line to be king. During their sojourn in the forest, Sita is abducted by the evil demon Ravana, and taken to his kingdom of Lanka. Rama journeys to Lanka and, with the help of the Monkey God Hanuman, succeeds in killing Ravana and rescues Sita. Rama's return from exile is celebrated across the country as Diwali, the Hindu festival of lights. He is crowned king on his return to Ayodhya. However, Rama's subjects raise doubts about Sita's moral character when they learn that she is pregnant. She is exiled to the forest where she gives birth to twin boys, Luv and Kush. She returns to Rama 15 years later, but when doubts about her character persist, she calls on Mother Earth to prove her innocence. In response, the earth opens up and swallows her.

A DIFFERENT VERSION OF THE RAMAYANA

The *Ramayana* has been translated into different Indian languages and given a variety of interpretations. The best-known version is the one provided by 16th century poet Tulsidas, who wrote *Ramcharitmanas* in Hindi. Tulsidas was unhappy with the Valmiki version of the Hindu epic and concluded his narration with Rama and Sita living happily ever after in Ayodhya.

MAHABHARATA

One of the two Hindu epics, the *Mahabharata* is a tale of war that took place between two branches of a royal family—the five Pandava brothers and their 100 cousins, the Kauravas—at Kurukshetra, near Delhi. Written about a century after the *Ramayana*, it is divided into 18 books and consists of 220,000 lines, making it the longest poem in the world. According to legend, a sage named Vyasa dictated the *Mahabharata* to the Elephant God, Ganesha, who then put it to paper.

The Pandavas are the sons of Dhritarashtra, while their cousins are the offspring of Dhritarashtra's younger brother Pandu. Pandu becomes king because Dhritarashtra is blind, but the cousins fight among themselves over succession to the throne. The Pandavas eventually lose the kingdom during a game and are banished to the forest for 13 years. The great war between the Pandavas and the Kauravas takes place after their return from the forest. The Pandavas win after an 18-day war and ascend the throne with Draupadi, who is married to all of them.

Like the *Ramayana*, the *Mahabharata* has a theme of good versus evil and salutes courage and faith. It upholds the honour of women through the example of Draupadi who is saved by the Hindu god Krishna from being publicly disrobed. She finds herself in this ordeal when Yudhisthira, king of the Pandavas, gambles her away during a contest with the Kauravas. Draupadi's honour is avenged when the Pandavas defeat the Kauravas. It is an invaluable source of Hindu cultural mores, mythology and philosophical thought from this period of Indian history.

The Bhagavad Gita

The sixth book of the *Mahabharata* contains the *Bhagavad Gita* or *Song of the Lord*, a significant Hindu text that preaches loyalty to God and the benefits of duty, knowledge, work and devotion, which are paths to salvation. The *Bhagavad Gita* is composed in the form of a dialogue between Prince Arjuna, one of the Pandavas, before he joins his brothers in the war with the Kauravas, and Hindu God Krishna in the guise of a charioteer. Arjuna is consumed by self-doubt on the Kurukshetra battlefield and tormented by the bloodshed. He pours out his anguish to Krishna and discusses the need for war with him. Krishna, who is a neutral party in the family dispute, advises detachment from the external world, which is illusory. The philosophy of Hinduism is presented comprehensively in this dialogue that is perceived as a message from God. The *Bhagavad Gita* is an invaluable guidebook for followers of Hinduism to cope with life's travails.

Shakuntala

Abhijnana Shakuntala (*Recognition of Shakuntala*), an all-time classic of world literature, was written by preeminent poet and playwright Kalidasa in the 4th century. It borrows the character of Shakuntala, a forest nymph, from the *Mahabharata* but develops it in a completely different way from the epic, dealing instead with delicacy and romance, anguish, pathos and happiness, culminating in a happy ending.

The play relates the story of Shakuntala, who lives in a hermitage and captures the heart of King Dushyanta while he is out hunting in the forest. They get married, but the king eventually leaves her to return to his palace. Before departing, he presents her his royal ring promising that he will return soon. Shakuntala spends the ensuing days pining for the king. In one of her dreamy states, she offends a visiting sage who curses that the person Shakuntala was thinking about would forget her. Later, he softens the curse by pronouncing that the king would remember her if he saw the ring. When Shakuntala discovers that she is expecting the king's child, she sets out for the palace but loses the ring while bathing in a lake. The king, without the evidence of the ring, does not remember her, and she returns forlorn to the forest where she delivers a baby boy. Years later, the king encounters the ring when a fisherman finds it inside a fish and presents it to him. The king instantly remembers Shakuntala and returns to the forest where he is reunited with her.

MODERN LITERATURE

Nobel Laureate Rabindranath Tagore (1861–1941)

The scion of an illustrious and wealthy Bengali family, Rabindranath Tagore was a poet and writer par excellence and one of the first modernists of his time. A cultural icon of his native Bengal, he wrote in a more colloquial form of the Bengali language, giving its literature a contemporary voice. His writing was meditative and contemplative and explored topical themes such as Indian nationalism and religious zeal. In *Ghare-Baire* (*The Home and the World*), for example, the hero Nikhil criticises the excesses committed by nationalists in the early 20th century. Another novel, *Gora*, is a study of the Indian identity and personal freedom in the context of a family relationship and a love triangle. *Ghare-Baire* was made into a film by renowned Bengali filmmaker Satyajit Ray.

The gifted Tagore, who was also a visual artist, composer, playwright and painter, became India's and Asia's first Nobel Laureate when he won the Nobel Prize for Literature in 1913, for *Gitanjali* (*Song Offerings*), a collection of poems that he had translated into English. He was knighted by the British Crown in 1915 but returned the honour a few years later in protest against British policies in India.

Tagore wrote in all the literary genres but was best known for his poetry, notably *Manasi* (*The Ideal One*), a collection of some of his best poems and social and political satire; *Sonar Tari* (*The Golden Boat*); *Gitimalya* (*Wreath of Songs*) and *Balaka* (*The Flight of Cranes*). Besides novels and short stories, Tagore also wrote musical dramas, dance dramas, essays, travel diaries, two autobiographies and songs for which he composed the music himself. At the age of almost 70, Tagore took up painting and produced some highly acclaimed works, making a name for himself in this creative field too.

INDIAN NATIONAL ANTHEM COMPOSED BY TAGORE

India's national anthem, *Jana Gana Mana*, was one of the many songs composed by Rabindranath Tagore. It was originally written in Bengali and was first sung on 27 December 1911 at the Calcutta meeting of the Indian National Congress party. The Hindi version of the song was adopted by the Constituent Assembly as the national anthem of India on 24 January 1950, two days before India was declared a republic.

Premchand (1880–1936)

The Indian literary tradition shifted from the subjects of gods and kings in ancient and medieval times to explore real-life issues such as social reform, caste and class tensions, conflicts, poverty, corruption and family themes, including the plight of widows, in the early 20th century. Munshi Premchand, born Dhanpat

Rai Srivastava, was one of the harbingers of this genre, pioneering fiction with a social purpose. He departed from the mythical and escapist literature prevalent at the time to write about the realities of the common man in rural India.

Writing in simple prose in Hindi and Urdu, Premchand composed stories from his own experiences, without the frills of popular literature. His last novel, *Godaan* (*The Gift of a Cow*), is considered the best of his extensive body of writing that includes 250 short stories, plays and more than a dozen novels. In *Godaan*, Hori, a poor peasant, desperately longs for a cow, which he believes will make him rich in his village. He does eventually get a cow but pays for it with his life.

Premchand's other noteworthy works include *Gaban* (*Embezzlement*), *Sevasadan* (*House of Service*) and *Nirmala* among the novels, and *Sadgati* (*Salvation*) and *Shatranj ke Khiladi* (*The Chess Players*) among the short stories. *Gaban*, *Shatranj ke Khiladi* and *Sevasadan* have been made into feature films, while *Sadgati* has been produced for television.

Booker Prize-Winning Novels

It was in 1981 that India-born Salman Rushdie won the highly coveted Booker Prize for *Midnight's Children*, his portrayal of India after it gained independence in 1947. Since then two other Indian writers have claimed the prize, Arundhati Roy in 1997 for *The God of Small Things* and Kiran Desai for *The Inheritance of Loss* in 2006. The three belong to an elite group of Indian writers who have earned international acclaim for their part-autobiographical, part-fictional novels that present India and Indians through the prism of their unique experiences.

Rushdie's Booker Prize-winning novel relates the story of Saleem Sinai, who was born at midnight on 15 August 1947, at the exact time when India broke free from British colonial rule. (Rushdie himself was born in Mumbai in June 1947.) Written in what has been called magic realism because of the way it merges the supernatural with the realistic, Rushdie attempts, through the unfolding of Saleem Sinai's life, to trace the developments in the tumultous Indian subcontinent after its partition and his own childhood years spent in Mumbai. The novel was also awarded the Booker of Bookers Prize in 1993 and made it to *Time* magazine's prestigious list of the 100 best English-language novels since 1923. Other books by Rushdie include *Shame*, the highly controversial *The Satanic Verses* and *The Moor's Last Sigh*. In subsequent works, Rushdie has explored Indian, Pakistani and Western themes, but *Midnight's Children* is considered his best work so far.

Arundhati Roy's *The God of Small Things* was her first book and is the only novel she has written. Set in the 1960s in a small town in Kerala, *The God of Small Things* relates the story of fraternal twins Rahel and Estha, and their family, from the perspective of seven-year-old Rahel. The two live with their mother, Ammu, their grandmother, uncle and grandaunt. The family owns a pickle factory and comes into conflict with the Communists over it. A pivotal event for the children is the tragic drowning of their visiting half-English cousin, Sophie Mol. The twins are separated and Rahel returns to the village at the age of 31 to find a decaying house and a fragmented family. This politically charged novel reveals interesting nuances of life in the Syrian Christian community in Kerala. It delves into the destructive aspects of the caste system as portrayed by Ammu's affair with a man from a lower caste.

Since winning the Booker Prize in 1997, Roy has turned activist and written about political issues close to her heart. Her subsequent works include *The Algebra of Infinite Justice*, a collection of essays, and *The Greater Common Good*, dealing with concerns such as the Narmada Dam project and India's nuclear weapons.

Kiran Desai's Booker Prize-winning *The Inheritance of Loss* is the writer's second novel, written while she was studying creative writing at Columbia University. Her first novel, *Hullabaloo in the Guava Orchard*, was critically acclaimed and received the Betty Trask Award for authors from Commonwealth countries. Kiran Desai is the daughter of Anita Desai, a distinguished author herself, who has been shortlisted for the Booker Prize three times but has never won it.

The Inheritance of Loss, described as 'a radiant, funny and moving family saga' by the Booker Prize judges, is set in the foothills of Mount Kanchenjunga in Kalimpong, India. It relates the story of a cranky old judge who wants nothing more than to be left alone to live in peace. But the arrival of his orphaned granddaughter, Sai, and her budding romance with her tutor shatters this desire. The story is complicated by the threat of an insurgency in neighbouring Nepal. The judge is forced to revisit his past, to try to make some sense of the present.

FOLKTALES AND PROVERBS

PANCHATANTRA

Indian culture is imbued with the colour and richness of folktales and fables. The tales of fantasy involving gods, humans, as well as animals who can talk, represent the diversity of ethnic groups and religions in the country. Many of the tales impart moral values and contain advice that both adults and children can use in their daily lives. The stories of *Panchatantra* (meaning 'Five Books') are among the oldest and the most popular folktales in the country and have even found their way to different corners of the world. They are believed to have reached Persia, Arabia and Greece through traders and travellers in ancient times. The *Panchatantra Tales* have been translated into more than 50 languages.

According to legend, the original tales were written by a learned Brahmin, Pandit Vishnu Sharma, in the Sanskrit language around 200 BC; their origin may, however, go back to the ancient Vedic period (1700 BC–500 BC). Most of the characters in the tales are animals, and each story has an interesting moral. The storyteller has set a story within a story, weaving an intriguing plot that keeps the reader guessing until the end. Pandit Vishnu Sharma wrote the stories to teach statecraft, philosophy, psychology, friendship and the art of relationships to the three foolish sons of King Amarshakti, ruler of a southern state in ancient India. By the end of their training, the ignorant princes had become wise and learned in the ways of the world.

The *Panchatantra Tales* are divided into five sections: Conflict Amongst Friends, Winning of Friends, Crows and Owls, The Forfeit of Profits and Action Without Due Consideration. Among the most popular *Panchatantra* tales are: 'The Cobra and the Crow', 'The Heron and the Crab', 'The Brahmin's Dream', 'The Lake of the Moon', 'The Brahmin and the Goat', 'The Crafty Jackal' and 'The Three Fishes'.

The Heron and the Crab

There was a lake in a jungle where lived a heron and many other creatures. The heron had grown old and didn't have the strength to catch fish. One day when he was starving, he came to the edge of the pond and began to cry. A crab came up to him and asked him why he was crying. The heron explained that he had heard from an astrologer that there would be no rain in the area for the next 12 years. Because of this, the lake would dry up and all the creatures in it would die. The heron said he was crying because all the creatures would die and nothing would be the same. The crab related this news to the other creatures and panic spread in the lake. The creatures went to consult the heron about what they could do to escape the drought. The heron told them that there was a lake nearby that had many lotus flowers and would never dry up. He offered to transport all the creatures to this lake; so one by one, they clambered onto his back. After flying a short distance, the heron would land on a rock, kill them and eat them up before flying back to get more.

Soon came the turn of the crab. As usual, the heron took the crab on his back and carried him to the rock where he had killed and eaten all the fish. The wily crab saw the bones and realised what the heron had been up to. He decided to trick the heron into talking while he moved up his back. Before the heron landed on the rock, the crab put his claws around the bird's neck and strangled him to death. Then he cut the heron's head off and dragged it back to the lake. There he told all the fish and other creatures how the heron had tricked them all.

Moral: An enemy can be destroyed by a trick.

THE JATAKA TALES

The *Jataka Tales* are stories about the life of the Buddha and are part of the Pali Canon, which is the name given to sacred Buddhist literature. The Pali Canon, established in c.486 BC at the first Buddhist council, contains the earliest Buddhist literature. For Theravada Buddhists, it represents the most authoritative of the sacred texts. Like the *Panchatantra Tales*, the *Jataka Tales* relate stories of animals, which represent the Buddha's former births in various forms. The Buddha is the central character in each story with a moral at the end. The stories were transmitted orally for centuries until they were finally penned in a combination of prose and verse. The 'Tale of the Two Parrots' is one of the popular *Jataka Tales*. In this story, the Buddha is the wise parrot, Radha.

The Tale of the Two Parrots

There were once two parrots, Radha and Potthapada, who loved to travel in search of food and new places to visit. One day, they entered the palace garden and were caught in a bird trap. The king was so fascinated by the birds that he ordered that they be kept in a special cage made of gold and fed special food every day.

Life was very comfortable for the two until a huge ape, Kalabahu, arrived at the palace. Guests and palace officials transferred their attention from the birds to the ape and he became the centre of attraction. Potthapada, the younger of the two parrots, was upset at being neglected and told his brother that they should leave the palace. But his brother, the wiser of the two, predicted that everyone would soon tire of the ape and their life would get back to normal. And that is exactly what happened. The birds were soon back in favour and people started disliking the ape for misbehaving.

Moral: True worth and ability ultimately get their due.

KATHASARITSAGARA

Another famous Indian collection of stories is grouped under the title *Kathasaritsagara* (*The Ocean of the Streams of Story*). This collection of tales and legends featuring gods, kings, humans and animals was written in Sanskrit in the 11th century by Somadeva, a writer from the northern state of Kashmir. It is said that he wrote the stories to entertain Queen Suryamati, the wife of King Ananta of Kashmir, who was despondent at the discontent and political intrigue rampant during that period. The collection of 18 books contains many stories interspersed with riddles that carry a message.

The Heads that Got Switched

This is a riddle within the story of 'King Vikramaditya and the Corpse'. Dhavala is a washerman who is married to Madanasundari, the daughter of another washerman. One day, Madanasundari's brother visits them and all three go to the temple of Goddess Parvati. Dhavala enters the temple empty-handed and beheads himself with the sacrificial sword as an offering to the goddess. When Madanasundari's brother discovers Dhavala's corpse, he beheads himself in anguish with the same sword. Madanasundari decides to kill herself too, but the goddess stops her and allows her to reattach the heads of the two men to their bodies and thus bring them back to life. Unfortunately, Madanasundari gets the two heads mixed up. The story ends with a riddle: which one of the two men is now Madanasundari's husband? The king replies that the man with Dhavala's head is her husband because the head rules the body, affirming the superiority of intellect over all else.

BIRBAL TALES

The *Birbal Tales* is a collection of stories about Birbal and Mughal Emperor Akbar in the 16th century. Birbal was one of the nine gems in Akbar's court, a member of his inner council of advisors renowned for his incredible wit. Exchanges between Birbal and Akbar have been recorded and passed down from generation to generation as folktales.

PROVERBS

Besides folktales, India also has an abundance of proverbs, many of which have their origin in ancient history. Proverbs are used regularly in daily conversation and, in earlier days, were sung by women as they went about their household chores. Native speakers might even use them to emphasise their point of view during a heated discussion.

> *Sari Ramayana sun-ke puchha Sita kis ki joru thi?*
> Translation: After listening to the whole *Ramayana*, he asks whose wife Sita was.

This saying expresses annoyance with someone who, after listening to an entire discourse, asks a most fundamental question, revealing that he was either distracted or is so stupid that he did not understand the basic facts. It refers to the Hindu epic the *Ramayana*, which is well-known to every Indian. This saying essentially pokes fun at a person for his ignorance.

> *Duba bans Kabir ka jo upja put Kamal.*
> Translation: The race of Kabir became extinct when his son Kamal was born.

This expression refers to the Indian mystic Kabir, a 15th-century Indian saint, known for his devotion to God and his poetry and lyrics espousing his universal spiritual teachings. When Kabir's son Kamal was still an infant, he guided the child according to his policy of universal benevolence and taught him to treat all mankind as one. Kabir suggested that Kamal look upon all women as his mother, sister or daughter. When Kamal came of age, Kabir asked him to look for a wife. Kamal responded by asking how he could marry his mother, sister or daughter, since the world comprised only these categories of women. He refused to get married and thus brought an end to the family lineage.

Ya base Gujar, ya rahe ujar.
Translation: May Gujars live here or else may
it remain uninhabited.
(Gujars are members of the northern Indian Gujar tribe.)

According to myth, when the monarch of Delhi, Ghiyas ud-din Tughlaq, was building his fort at Tughlaqabad, near Delhi, Sufi saint Nizamuddin Aulea began to sink a well in its vicinity, which disrupted the work at the fort. The king, annoyed at this affront, immediately ordered all the workers to stop work at the well and to focus their energies on the construction of the fort. This only spurred the workers to split the tasks, and they worked at the fort during the day and at the well at night. One day, when the king observed workers at the fort site sleeping during the day, he questioned them closely and learned the truth. Further incensed, he ordered all the shopkeepers in the area to stop selling oil for the lamps to Nizamuddin. But even this move failed to deter the Sufi saint from completing the work on his well. Fed up with the situation, the king ordered Nizamuddin to be executed, to which the saint reacted by pronouncing a curse: "May lightning strike Tughlaq; may Gujars live in his fort or it remain uninhabited." Soon after, the king was struck by lightning and since then, the fort has fallen to ruin, inhabited partially by Gujars and low caste Muslims.

Ninnanve ghare dudh men ek ghara pani kiya jana jae.
Translation: A pitcher of water cannot be noticed
among 99 pitchers of milk.

This saying has its origins in the court of Mughal Emperor Akbar. According to legend, Akbar asked his minister Birbal which was the most untrustworthy class in the kingdom. Birbal replied that milkmen were not to be trusted. To prove his point, he ordered all the milkmen to fill a tank with pure milk by pouring a pitcher of milk each into the tank. Each milkman poured in a pitcher of water instead, thinking to himself that no one would find out that he had put water in the tank of milk. When Akbar went to see the tank, it was filled with pure water, thus proving Birbal's surmise.

ARTS AND
CRAFTS

Indian art dates back to the Mesolithic period in prehistoric times in the form of simple rock carvings at Bhimbetka, south of the city of Bhopal. The Neolithic peoples of Mehrgarh followed with their seals and ceramic pottery. Painted earthenware and seals, significant because of their clearly defined figures of animals such as the elephant, buffalo and tiger, emerged from the Indus Valley Civilisation. Figures of human beings and animals made of baked clay and bronze have also been found from this period, indicating a highly developed culture and an awareness of human and animal forms.

Since those early days, art has flourished in every region of India, with each state possessing its own distinct style and specialty that has evolved from different historical and religious influences, as well as the skills and raw materials predominant in the area. Different techniques, colours and media are used to depict local deities and other religious themes, as well as scenes from daily life, fairs, festivals and legends.

MADHUBANI PAINTING

From the northern state of Bihar comes Madhubani, a style of folk art that derives its name from the town of Madhuban. It was originally created by women on the freshly plastered mud walls of huts using rice paste and vegetable colours. Over the years, this style of painting has found expression on handmade paper, canvas and even cloth. The works represent major Hindu gods and goddesses, festivals, marriage, the cycle of life and death and figures from nature and mythology in vibrant colours. The art is also symbolic—a fish is depicted to signify good luck and serpents represent the protector.

CAVE ART

The Gupta emperors, who reigned during the 4th to 6th centuries, were major patrons of art and literature, and encouraged both to flourish. In fact, the Gupta period is referred to as the Golden Age of Indian art and culture—even the Gupta coins were artistically made. During this period, Buddhist, Jain and Hindu styles converged, and angular figures such as the image of the Hindu god Vishnu, in a boar incarnation, took on softer lines. Many of the famous Ajanta caves, a UNESCO World Heritage Site, were built during the Gupta period. The oldest caves date from the 1st and 2nd centuries BC.

Buddhism had an early influence on Indian art, and some of the best known examples of this are found at the Ajanta caves, north-east of Mumbai in the western Indian state of Maharashtra. The 30 caves, carved out of rock, are adorned with sculptures and paintings depicting the Buddha's life and Buddhist legends and are considered masterpieces. Near Ajanta are the Ellora caves, first built in the 7th century. These caves have rock carvings created by Buddhist, Hindu, and Jain sculptors with the application of mud and lime plaster. The pigments for the bright colours used came from local volcanic rocks, and the glue came from animal and vegetable sources.

TEMPLE ARCHITECTURE

India's multitudinous temples are a prominent showcase of the country's diverse religions, as well as its rich art heritage. Hindu temples are particularly notable for their intricate carving and sculpture and their contrasting architecture, which is broadly classified under the predominant Nagara and Dravidian styles. Typically, Nagara architecture prevails in north India, while in the south, temples are built according to the Dravidian style.

Temples built in the Nagara style have a beehive-shaped layered tower, a notable example being the Hindu and Jain temple complex at Khajuraho, Madhya Pradesh. The complex is divided into the western, eastern and southern temples; the western group has been designated a UNESCO

World Heritage Site. The temples are famous for their sculptures depicting gods and goddesses, as well as *apsaras* (nymphs) in different postures. Some of the sculptures have an erotic theme with their depiction of amorous couples. The Temple of Kandariya particularly abounds with sculptures that have been described as masterpieces of Indian art. Today, only about 20 temples, built during the 10th and 11th centuries, remain in the famous Khajuraho complex.

The ancient kingdom of Kalinga, now Orissa, is also renowned for its magnificent temples, especially the Lingaraja Temple in Bhubaneswar. Built around 1000, it has been acclaimed as one of the finest Hindu temples in India. It stands in a cluster of small shrines and is dominated by its tower known as the *vimana*, which is topped by figures representing a lion crushing an elephant.

The Dravidian temples have a pyramid-shaped tower topped by a dome. They differ markedly from the northern temples in the style of the gateways. In the north, the gateway is usually modest, while in the south, gateways are tall, elaborate structures called *gopurams*, which sometimes dominate the whole temple site. A noteworthy example of a Dravidian-style temple is the Meenakshi Sundareswarar temple in Madurai, one of the biggest temples in India. It is adorned with intricate carvings and sculptures and has 12 massive *gopurams*.

GLASS PAINTING

Glass painting originated from southern India during the 16th century where it was employed in the courts of the kings of Tanjore in Tamil Nadu. A popular subject was the Hindu god Krishna, depicted in a variety of poses. These opulent paintings were done on glass and board and were heavily decorated with semi-precious stones, beaten gold leaf and gilt metal. The stones were stuck on the image with a mixture of sawdust and glue. The skill of the craftsmen lay in the effective balancing of the stones.

MINIATURE PAINTINGS

Mughal Emperor Akbar (1542–1605) encouraged artists to create miniature paintings portraying scenes from history, rural and urban life, animals and religious themes that were inspired by Persian art, yet rooted in the local environment. Even literary works produced during his reign, such as the *Akbar Nama* and the *Razm Nama*, were heavily illustrated at his behest. Other schools of miniature paintings include the Rajput and the Deccan styles.

Rajput miniature paintings, practised in the states of Bengal, Bihar, Orissa, Gujarat, Himachal Pradesh, Madhya Pradesh and Rajasthan from the 16th to the 19th centuries, were related to Mughal painting and other early styles. Vegetable dyes were used to create distinctive paintings dominated by motifs from nature and graceful human figures depicting Buddhist and Jain themes, as well as scenes from the *Ramayana* and the *Mahabharata*. This art form exists even today and is a popular tourist attraction.

FOLK ART

Other painting styles prevalent in India include *kalamkari* from southern India, *pata* from Orissa state, *phad* from Rajasthan state and *thanka* from Ladakh. *Kalamkari* is an ancient craft that uses hand painting and block printing with vegetable dyes, while *pata* is a tradition in which either cotton or silk cloth is treated with a combination of gum, chalk and tamarind to give it a leathery appearance. It depicts religious themes. *Phad* from Rajasthan state is characterised by bright colours painted on cloth to depict historic tales of local leaders, and *thanka* is a style of painting with vivid colours with a Buddhist theme painstakingly created on silk or cotton. These paintings are dominated by forms of the dragon.

The rich traditions of Indian art declined during British rule, a period in which Indian artists adapted modern Western techniques to produce works that would appeal to Europeans. Nobel literature laureate Rabindranath Tagore, who was also a visual artist, introduced Asian and avant-garde Western styles into Indian art. The Progressive Artists Group (PAG), founded in 1947 by a group of six artists, among them Maqbool Fida Husain, further changed the direction of Indian art. It was with the vital contribution made by the PAG that modern Indian art developed a new form and image.

PAINTING WITH HENNA

Painting with henna paste, made from the henna plant (botanical name *Lawsonia inermis*), is an ancient Indian practice used during festivals, dance performances and special occasions such as marriages to decorate the hands and feet. The leaves of the plant are ground into a paste that is applied to the palms, back of the hand and the top of the feet through a conical applicator, usually made of thick paper. The designs are fine and intricate, and geometric shapes and floral motifs from Indian art are most commonly used. The henna is left to dry, then washed or scraped off to leave an orange-red coloured design. The pigmentation stays for several days, reinforced with the application of oil, but fades away eventually. Known to be a coolant, henna is also used for medicinal purposes and as a nourishing hair colouring.

MODERN ART

Over the years, the trend in art has shifted to the adaptation of traditional imagery and ideas to modern styles such as Impressionism, Futurism, Cubism and Surrealism. With some artists adopting modern techniques, some continuing to create traditional folk and tribal art and others taking inspiration from old traditions, contemporary Indian art has become rich and highly diverse and is much sought after the world over.

While Indian artists in bygone years often dedicated their art to the divine and, as such, did not feel the need to affix their signatures to their works, modern artists are not averse to having their art acknowledged and appreciated. In fact, modern Indian artists such as Nandalal Bose, Jamini Roy, Amrita Sher-Gil, N S Bendre, M B Samant, Maqbool Fida Husain, Krishen Khanna, Satish Gujral, Tyeb Mehta, Bhupen Khakhar and Vasudeo Gaitonde have a large following in India as well as overseas. Museums, art institutions and art dealers have been showing considerable interest in contemporary Indian art, and buyers are increasingly looking upon it as a good investment. The Indian government, through the National Academy of Arts, has helped popularise Indian art abroad by actively participating in international biennales and other events.

DOYEN OF MODERN INDIAN PAINTING

Maqbool Fida Husain is India's most renowned modern artist and one of its most prolific. The 91-year-old, known for his eccentric ways, is also a filmmaker, having made his first film, *Through the Eyes of a Painter*, in 1967.

Husain was born in 1915 in Pandharpur, Maharashtra, and moved to Mumbai at the age of 20, where he had his first taste of formal training in art at the JJ School of Arts. To make ends meet, the young Husain painted cinema hoardings, which gave him valuable training in painting on a large canvas.

His early paintings displayed images of mothers with children and toiling peasants in earthy colours, while later works were more mythical. His painting *Yatra* (1955) shows a rural family driven to pilgrimage by the Hindu Monkey God Hanuman. In the 1960s–1970s, he painted dancers, musicians and horses and explored mythical themes from the *Ramayana* and the *Mahabharata*. The 1980s saw a moving series on Mother Teresa and the *Portrait of an Umbrella* series, which dealt with the lives of ordinary people.

In recent years, he has gone back to films, making *Gajagamini* and *Minaxi—A Tale of Three Cities*, and is planning a comedy for his fourth film. The painter-turned-filmmaker remains one of India's most prolific artists despite his advancing age. He painted a suite of 88 paintings of different cities to commemorate his 88th birthday.

CLAY, WOOD, STONE AND METALWARE

As with paintings, the different regions and states of India have their unique styles of handicrafts fashioned from a variety of materials and intricate designs handed down from generation to generation. The creativity of the local folk finds expression in clay, stone, brass, copper, bronze, wood and ivory, in objects that are utilitarian, ritualistic or purely decorative.

Terracotta, hard semi-fired ceramic clay, is used to create figurines with a ritualistic symbolism, as in the case of the famous Bankura horse from the state of West Bengal. The horse derives its name from the Bankura district of the state and forms an important part of rituals. The rider is the local god, Dharmaraj, seen as another form of Surya, the Sun God who is a rider of horses. The four legs of the horse are made first, followed by the torso, neck and head, after which the different parts are glued together. The figure, once dry, is coloured and burnt in the kiln. The size of the horse can vary from 15 cm to 1.8 m. Besides terracotta, the Bankura horse is also made in wood.

Wood is another popular medium for Indian handicrafts with the tradition of woodcarving dating back to ancient times. From Punjab and Kashmir in the north, Nagaland in the east, to Andhra Pradesh, Kerala, and Tamil Nadu in the south, wood is used to create objects as varied as dolls, boxes, furniture, screens, decorative panels and idols of local gods. In some parts of India such as Karnataka, wood is combined with other materials like ivory or metal thread to create exquisite designs.

Stone carving developed after woodcarving in India but is no less popular. Intricate inlay work is done using black marble and soapstone. The city of Agra, home to the marble edifice the Taj Mahal, is famous for its marble crafts, while in neighbouring Jaipur, carvers are known for their stone-and-marble deities, among other objects of art and worship. Even windows and door frames are made of carved stones in Agra.

The city of Moradabad in Uttar Pradesh is famous for brass. Brass is created by fusing zinc and copper and is used to make everything from flower vases, pots and figurines to utility items such as nut crackers and storage boxes. In the southern city of Hyderabad, brass is inlaid in an alloy of silver and copper to create the decorative *bidri* work. Copper, silver and brass are fashioned into samovars, glasses and water jugs for practical and decorative use even in the remote northern region of Ladakh. Bronze is another favourite metal, dating back to ancient times, and is widely used across Indian states for creating figures of deities, usually Shiva, Ganesha and Rama.

RANGOLI: PAINTING ON FLOORS

The powder of rice flour and lime or stone, coloured with dye, is used to decorate floors during festive occasions such as Diwali, the Festival of Lights, in India. The designs, either geometrical or based on floral, animal and spiritual motifs, are traditionally applied by hand at the entrance of the home to welcome guests, or to seek blessings from the gods. The designs are usually symmetrical in nature. They are drawn on the floor with chalk, then powder is taken between the thumb and index finger and sprinkled on the design, filling it in carefully. Powders of different colours are kept separate to create a distinct design. Flower petals, candles or earthenware lamps are often added to create a more pleasing look.

PERFORMING ARTS

BOLLYWOOD: THE DREAM MACHINE

With a total production rate of over 1,000 films a year, the Indian film industry is undoubtedly the largest celluloid dream-spinner in the world, even bigger than the American Hollywood, which makes about 400 movies annually. The Indian film industry is a conglomerate of films from different states in the country, but it is the Hindi industry, called Bollywood after Hollywood, that accounts for about 20 per cent of total production and dominates both in terms of nationwide popularity and production.

The themes of commercial Indian films vary from the mythological to the romantic, historical and patriotic to comic, action and horror. The bulk, however, are a pot-pourri of family drama, romance and action, laced with numerous songs performed by the actors but sung by playback singers. Unlike Hollywood productions, Indian films avoid nudity and overt sex scenes—until a few years ago even passionate kissing on screen was taboo—because of state censorship and, in some cases, self-censorship imposed by the filmmakers themselves.

The first feature film to be made in India was *Raja Harishchandra*, based on the Hindu epic, the *Mahabharata*. The film, made by Dhundiraj Govind Phalke, better known as Dadasaheb Phalke, tells the story of an honest king who loses his kingdom. It was screened in 1913. Phalke's film was a success and it ran for a month in Mumbai. For his contribution to Indian cinema, Phalke is referred to as the 'Father of Indian Cinema'.

Sound came to Indian cinema in 1931 with *Alam Ara* (*Beauty of the World*). The film, produced by Ardeshir Irani, had seven songs and introduced the song-and-dance routine, which has become a key part of Indian cinema. Sound brought with it complications related to language, and given the vast number of languages spoken in multilingual India, another consideration for Mumbai filmmakers was which language to produce their films in. Hindi, or a type of spoken Hindi called Hindustani, emerged as the language that offered the biggest market.

Playback singing, a technique in which a song is recorded in advance and the actor lip-syncs the lyrics on screen, was introduced in 1935, transforming the fledgling Hindi film industry. Playback singing soon became the norm and gave rise to playback singers who, along with the actors and actresses, became celebrities in their own right. Singers who made their mark at that time and continued to dominate playback singing in Mumbai for years to come include Mukesh, Mohammad Rafi, Kishore Kumar among the male vocalists, and Lata Mangeshkar and Asha Bhonsle among the female vocalists.

Filmmaking in those early years included rural dramas with social and political themes, biographical films about popular historical figures and films adapted from literature. Independence from British rule in 1947 brought in its wake a desire for nation-building, but the euphoria was shortlived when filmmakers found the new government giving the film industry a back seat in its push for industrialisation and economic development. The government also tightened censorship and imposed heavy taxes, viewing the industry as a key source of revenue. Nevertheless, this period saw a proliferation of films with patriotic themes.

It was some decades later, in the early 1970s, that the 'angry young man' entered Hindi cinema and transformed the image of the soft, romantic hero popular at the time. It was the huge success of the 1973 film *Zanjeer* (*Chain*), starring Amitabh Bachchan as a police officer who takes the law into his own hands, that shifted the focus from middle class, family-oriented themes to the larger arena of the society and state. Actors such as Bachchan,

Rajesh Khanna and Vinod Khanna were supported by heroines such as Rekha, Rakhee and Bollywood's quintessential 'Dream Girl', Hema Malini. However, the heroine was a mere wallflower, whose primary task was to stand by the hero's side till the end. Villains came to the fore in the formulaic good-versus-bad plots, playing smugglers, black marketeers and corrupt politicians, brought to justice by the zealous, do-good hero, who always 'gets his man'. Another popular theme at that time was the 'lost and found' family plot, where siblings are separated in their childhood and are reunited as adults for a happy ending.

Bollywood in Transition

The 1990s brought with it economic liberalisation and the entry of satellite television into India, two factors which had a huge impact on Bombay's film industry. By 1992, when Star TV and Zee TV, India's first private Hindi language satellite channels, were launched, the Indian entertainment landscape had changed drastically and Indian filmmakers were faced with real competition from the 'idiot box'. To entice audiences to leave their living rooms and watch movies in theatres, filmmakers began improving production values, and digital sound, foreign locations and elaborate sets became the order of the day. Globalisation and liberalisation brought about the internationalisation of the production and distribution of Indian films, and Hindi filmmakers made a concerted effort to seek overseas audiences. In fact, in recent years, some Hindi films have enjoyed greater commercial success among members of the Indian diaspora in countries such as Britain and the United States, than back home in India.

This period also saw a shift away from the angry young man and villain films to entertaining, family-oriented cinema, with an overlay of romance, family values and nationalism. There has also been a depiction of terrorism, with films like J. P. Dutta's 1997 *Border*, effectively tackling this issue. The mid-1990s saw an upsurge of big-budget flicks that combined love stories within family spectacles such as weddings. Most notable of these were *Hum Aapke Hain Koun* (*Who Am I to You*) and *Dilwale Dulhaniya Le Jayenge* (*The One with a Pure Heart will Get the Bride*). Shah Rukh Khan, originally a television actor, came into the spotlight during this period. Another family-oriented blockbuster of this decade was *Kuch Kuch Hota Hai* (*Something is Happening to Me*), a pot-pourri of romance, comedy, and entertainment revolving around a love triangle with a tragic twist. This movie further consolidated the star status enjoyed by Shah Rukh Khan, who has dominated Mumbai filmdom since the 1990s. Unlike the all-important hero in male-dominated Hindi films, leading ladies have not been able to sustain their hold over the box office. Madhuri Dixit held sway for a long while, giving way to Kajol and Juhi Chawla, who then passed the baton on to Preity Zinta, Rani Mukherji and Aishwarya Rai.

The 21st century has seen the advent of professionalism in Bollywood. It was in the year 2000 that the Indian government finally gave filmmaking the status of an industry. This paved the way for producers to get legitimate insurance and bank loans for their films, reducing the age-old reliance on illegitimate sources, including the notorious financiers of the underworld. India's corporations have also ventured into the media business, sponsoring television shows and looking to make a foray into films too.

Even as winds of change blow through Bollywood, its winning escapist formula combined with lavish sets, a generous dose of songs and dances, and a glamorous cast, continues to draw the crowds. As far as Bollywood is concerned, some things are unlikely to change.

BIG B AND KING KHAN

Countless heroes have come and gone since the birth of Bollywood but there has never been anyone quite like Amitabh Bachchan, or Big B, and Shah Rukh Khan or King Khan. Between the two of them, they have dominated Hindi filmdom for over three decades. Amitabh Bachchan still towers above Bollywood, despite his grey hair and advancing years, while Shah Rukh Khan remains the national heartthrob, his position unshaken even when he appears in a negative role. The two have starred together in big budget extravaganzas such as *Kabhi Khushi Kabhi Gham* (*Sometimes Happiness, Sometimes Sadness*) and *Kabhi Alvida Naa Kehna* (*Don't Ever Say Goodbye*), both box office hits.

MUSIC

Like art, music in diverse India is an eclectic mix of the classical and contemporary, folk and devotional. Classical music, which has its origins in the sacred Hindu text *Sama Veda*, can be broadly classified into the north Indian and south Indian traditions, with distinct nomenclature, instruments and styles of performance. The two, however, share the fundamental forms of Indian classical music—the *raga* (melody) and *tal* (rhythm). *Ragas*, which are meant to evoke the different human emotions, are made up of combinations of the seven notes of Indian music: *Sa Sadjam, Ri Rishab, Ga Gaandhaar, Ma Madhyam, Pa Pancham, Dha Dhaivad, Ni Nishad.*

Four types of instruments are used in Indian classical music—the *tantrum* (strings), *susir* (wind), *avanada* (percussion) and *Ghana* (gongs, bell and cymbal). Among the numerous Indian instruments in the strings category are the *sarangi, sarod, santoor* and *sitar.* The *tabla* is a percussion instrument, while the *shehnai* represents the wind category.

Carnatic music is devotional in nature with its lyrics addressed to any one of the many deities in the pantheon of Hindu deities. It has 62 basic roots known as the Melakarta Ragams, which in turn have seven notes—Sa, Re, Ga, Ma, Pa, Da and Ne. This system, divided into two sets of 31 *ragas*, is similar to the Western system of scales and flats.

Hindustani music has five different forms: Dhrupad, Dhamar, Khayal, Tappa and Thumri. Dhrupad is the oldest with traditional compositions praising the gods and monarchs, and also includes lyrics about nature. Khayal is the dominant form of contemporary art music and allows the singer greater flexibility and opportunities for creative improvisation.

Other forms of Indian music include Ghazal, Qawwali and folk music.

SITAR AND RAVI SHANKAR

The *sitar*, invented in the 13th century by Amir Khusro, is one of the most famous of Indian stringed instruments. It is made from seasoned gourd and teak wood and has about seven main strings and 13 others designed for sympathetic resonance. The *sitar* has been popularised around the world by its greatest exponent, maestro Ravi Shankar. Shankar is a musician and composer of great eminence who has won countless international awards, including two Grammys from the American Recording Academy, for his pioneering work in synthesising the music of the East and West.

DANCE

Like music, dance in India has traditionally been a form of worship of the gods, and all dance forms were structured around the nine emotions or *rasa*, namely, happiness, sorrow, anger, compassion, disgust, wonder, fear, courage and serenity. The main classical dance forms are Bharatanatyam, Kathak, Odissi, Kuchipudi, Mohiniattam, Manipuri and Kathakali. Indian folk dances include Chhau, Dandiya Raas, Garba and Bhangra.

It is believed that Indian classical dance was defined by sage Bharata Muni in the *Natya Shastra* (*Treatise of Dance*), written in Sanskrit sometime between 200 BC and 200 AD. Bharatanatyam is one of the oldest and most popular of the classical dances. It traces its origins to the Devadasi tradition prevalent in southern India in medieval times. Under the Devadasi tradition, women were dedicated to temples and danced for the deities. Bharatanatyam is primarily a solo dance and involves elaborate gestures and postures performed to Carnatic music. It has three main elements: *nritta*, the rhythmic movements of the body, feet and hands; *natya*, mime using facial gestures; and *nritya*, a combination of the two.

Folk Dances

Each region and village has its own folk dances performed during festivals and on special occasions such as weddings and the birth of a child. The dances are performed to seek blessings from gods, or to express joy and the spirit of celebration. Each dance has a distinct colourful costume, which is often worn with elaborate jewellery. Most of the dances are easy to perform and do not require extensive training, unlike the classical dances. Both men and women usually take part in folk dances, though the traditional form of Bhangra is performed primarily by men. Bhangra is a vigorous dance performed during the harvest festival of Baisakhi in Punjab state. The dancers are accompanied by a drummer who usually stands at the centre of the group.

DANDIYA AND GARBA

Energetic dances that originated in the western state of Gujarat, both Dandiya and Garba are performed in honour of the goddess Amba. The Garba is a fertility dance in which women carry oil lamps in pots on their heads and move around in a circle, balancing the pots. They snap their fingers and clap their hands to produce a fast beat. The dance was traditionally performed at night, but in its modern version, it is performed at any time.

In the Dandiya, the dancers carry colourful sticks which they use either solo or in partnership with other dancers. Here too, the dancers move in a circle and every time they move their sticks, the tiny bells on the sticks make a tinkling sound which adds to the pleasure of the dance.

INVENTIONS AND
MEDICINE

MATHEMATICS

India has an impressive track record in mathematics and science dating back to the ancient Indus Valley Civilisation (2800 BC–1900 BC). In fact, modern mathematics can trace its origins to India where the decimal system and the base-10 system with a symbol and a position for zero were discovered.

Historical records reveal that a basic version of the decimal system was in use during the Indus Valley Civilisation. Weights corresponding to ratios of 0.05, 0.1, 0.2, 0.5, 1, 2, 5, 10, 20, 50, 100, 200 and 500 have been identified from archaeological finds, as have scales with decimal divisions. A bronze rod marked in units of 0.367 inches, unearthed in present-day Pakistan, also suggests the advanced knowledge employed in town planning in that period.

The place value system was uncovered in the Vedic period of Indian history and is explained in detail in the ancient scriptures the Vedas. The units 10, 100 and 1,000 are named *daza, zata* and *sahasra* respectively in the Sanskrit language along with 10,000, 100,000, 10 million and 100 million (*ayuta, laksa, koti, vyarbuda*), up to the fifty-third power. By giving each power of ten an individual name, the Vedic system gave no special importance to any number. Later, in c.100 BC, Indian author Pingala described for the first time a system of binary enumeration convertible to decimal numerals in his *Chandas Shastra* treatise. His discovery bears similarities to the binary system developed much later by German polymath Gottfried Wilhelm Leibniz, in the 17th century.

India is also credited with the discovery of the numeral zero, disclosed in *Lokavibhaaga*, a text of the Jain religion which dates back to 458. The concept of zero, however, is believed to have appeared earlier, in the Babylonian number system. The workings of the Indian numeral system reached the Arabs in the 7th or 8th century and travelled to Europe in the 12th century. The Europeans, who were using the Roman numeral system at the time, were initially resistant to the Indian method, but adopted it eventually.

Aryabhata

At about the same time as the numeral zero was discovered in India, an astronomer, Aryabhata, proposed that the Earth was a sphere that spun on its axis. He ascribed the motion of the moon to the Earth's rotation. It was 499 and Aryabhata was only 23 years old. In his famous text on astronomy and mathematics, *Aaryabhatiiya*, he argued that the positions and periods of the planets were relative to a stationary Sun. He posited that the Moon and planets reflected sunlight, and that the orbits of the planets were ellipses around the Sun. Aryabhata computed the Earth's circumference as 39,736 km (24,835 miles), which was only 0.2 per cent smaller than the actual value of 39,843 km (24,902 miles). He calculated the length of the day as 23 hours, 56 minutes and 4.1 seconds; the modern value is 23:56:4.091. Similarly, he estimated the length of a year at 365.358 days—only 3 minutes and 20 seconds longer than the true value.

In mathematics, one of Aryabhata's greatest contributions was the calculation of sine tables which went into the realm of trigonometry. He also developed methods of solving quadratic and indeterminate equations using fractions, and calculated pi to four decimal places, i.e., 3.1416. Aryabhata's text was translated into Arabic and influenced the development of Arabic and European mathematics.

OTHER BRILLIANT MATHEMATICIANS

Other brilliant mathematicians of the classical age of Indian mathematics were Brahmagupta, Bhaaskara and Maadhava. Brahmagupta's best known work is the *Brahmasphuta Siddhanta*, written in 628, in which he developed a solution for a certain type of second order indeterminate equation.

Bhaaskara was an outstanding mathematician from south India. Born in 1114 in Karnataka, he composed a four-part text entitled *Siddhanta Ziromani*, which includes a significant section on algebra. It contains descriptions of advanced mathematical techniques involving both positive and negative integers, as well as zero and irrational numbers.

Maadhava made history with his writings on trigonometry. He calculated the sine, cosine and arctangent of the circle, developing the world's first consistent system of trigonometry.

Nobel Laureate C V Raman

One of the most famous scientists of modern India is Chandrasekhara Venkata (CV) Raman, who wrote scientific treatises on quantum mechanics, particularly the molecular scattering of light. Raman was awarded the Nobel Prize in Physics in 1930 for his discovery of the Raman Effect, which shows that the energy of a photon can undergo partial transformation within matter. A few years later, Raman, along with his colleague Nagendra Nath, propounded the Raman-Nath Theory on the diffraction of light by ultrasonic waves. He was a director of the Indian Institute of Science and founded the Indian Academy of Sciences in 1934 and the Raman Research Institute in 1948.

Another leading scientist of the 1900s was Homi Jehangir Bhabha, a physicist renowned for his contributions to the fields of positron theory and cosmic rays at the University of Cambridge in Britain. In 1945, Bhabha established the Tata Institute of Fundamental Research in Mumbai.

Other eminent Indian scientists include Sir Jagadish Chandra Bose, a Cambridge-educated Bengali physicist who discovered the application of electromagnetic waves to wireless telegraphy in 1895; Meghnad Saha, a nuclear physicist who gave new insight into the functions of stellar spectra; Satyendranath Bose, who collaborated with Albert Einstein in the 1920s to produce the Bose-Einstein Condensation Theory.

TRADITIONAL MEDICINE

India has a long tradition of natural cures and herbal medicines dating back to the Vedic period. Of the two homegrown systems of medicine in use in India, Ayurveda and Siddha, Ayurveda is the more popular. However, although it has been in use in India for more than 3,000 years, its methods have not yet found universal acceptance. It remains a complementary and alternative system of medicine in Western countries such as the United States, where it is used largely for its dietary and lifestyle related guidelines, mostly to support modern allopathic medicine. The Indian government is spearheading a drive to promote the healing powers of Ayurveda and other systems of traditional medicine around the world, and to establish the safety of its drugs through enhanced research and scientific testing.

Ayurveda

Ayurveda, which is the Sanskrit word for 'meaning of life', is a holistic system of medicine that first came to light in the *Vedas*. It is said to have divine origins, delivered to humanity by the Hindu god Brahma, the supreme creator. The Vedic scripture *Charka Samhita* is the most significant text on ancient medicine and contains several chapters dealing with therapeutic or internal medicine using 600 drugs of plant, animal and mineral origin. The *Sushruta Samhita* is another vital medical source and pertains to surgery, providing detailed descriptions of incisions, excision, extraction and bandaging. Ayurveda has eight disciplines: internal medicine, paediatrics, psychiatry, ophthalmology, surgery, toxicology, geriatrics and aphrodisiacs.

In the Ayurveda system of medicine, human beings—and all objects in the universe—consist of five elements: space, air, fire, water and earth. Two or more of these elements combine to produce specific reactions in us. For instance, space and air combine to form *vata dosha*, which directs nerve impulses, circulation, respiration and elimination. Fire and water combine to form pitta dosha, the process of metabolism. Finally, the water and earth elements combine to form the kapha dosha which controls growth.

According to Ayurvedic principles, each individual is made up of unique proportions of *vata*, *pitta* and *kapha*. A change in the natural equilibrium due to poor diet, lack of exercise or unhealthy habits can cause illness, and treatment seeks to restore the balance. Ayurveda offers principles of healthy living, as well as treatments for a variety of diseases ranging from common colds and influenza to the more severe illnesses, such as bronchial asthma, ischaemic heart disease, rheumatoid arthritis and acute viral hepatitis. The different Ayurvedic treatments include: purification, palliative treatment, diet, activity and psychotherapy. Massage, using special herbal oils, also plays a key role in this system of treatment.

One of the more commonly used ingredients of Ayurvedic medicine is turmeric, which is beneficial in the treatment of rheumatoid arthritis and Alzheimer's disease, and aids in wound healing. A combination of sulphur, iron, powdered dried fruits and tree root is also used to treat liver problems. An extract from the tropical shrub commiphora mukul, or guggul, has been used for several illnesses and seems to be effective in lowering cholesterol. The botanical plants used in Ayurvedic treatment are sometimes mixed with metals.

Ayurvedic methods and practices were widely employed to cure all kinds of ailments but suffered a long period of neglect during the period of Muslim invasions from the 11th to the 19th centuries. Ayurveda saw a revival in the early 20th century when Indian nationalists demanded government patronage for its development in accordance with modern scientific parameters. The movement gathered momentum after India's independence in 1947. The first tertiary institution to teach Ayurveda—the Ayurvedic and Unani Tibbia College—was inaugurated by Mahatma Gandhi in 1921. As Ayurveda received wider acceptance and official recognition, more and more institutions sprang up across the country. Finally in 1964–1965, the government set up the Central Board of Siddha and Ayurvedic Medicine to regulate this sector of medicine. Today, most major Indian cities have an Ayurvedic college and hospital. Institutions teaching Ayurveda can also be found in Europe and the United States.

THE HEALTH BENEFITS OF TURMERIC

Turmeric is an essential spice in India, used in curries and most vegetable and meat preparations. Besides its usefulness as a preservative and colouring in Indian cooking, its medicinal properties, particularly as an internal and external antiseptic, have long been acknowledged. Recent studies conducted in the West have reported the extensive benefits of turmeric in the fight against cancer. Curcumin, a compound in turmeric with antioxidant properties, has been found to inhibit melanoma cell growth and stimulate tumour cell death.

Siddha System of Medicine

The Siddha system of traditional Indian medicine shares principles and practices with Ayurveda. Siddha is practised largely in southern India by Tamil-speaking people and is therapeutic in nature. Textbooks written in the Tamil language provide a detailed classification of the different minerals and metals used in drug formulation. According to legend, the knowledge of Siddha originated with the Hindu god Shiva who passed it on to his consort, Parvati. It eventually found its way to the Siddhars, who were distinguished scientists in ancient times.

Siddha believes that the human body is composed of the five basic elements of earth, water, fire, air and sky, which are also found in food, medicines and everything else in the universe. Like Ayurveda, Siddha is a holistic system that uses a combination of metals and minerals in its drugs. It employs 25 varieties of water-soluble inorganic compounds, which are essentially different types of alkalis and salts, and 64 varieties of minerals that do not dissolve in water but emit vapours when placed in a fire. Sulphur and mercury occupy a crucial place in Siddha medicine, and items such as gold, silver, copper, lead and iron, incinerated by a special process, are used in making traditional medicines. Besides plant sources, Siddha also obtains drugs from animal sources.

The Siddha system is capable of treating all types of disease and is known to be particularly effective in treating urinary tract infections and diseases of the liver and the gastrointestinal tract. Siddha practitioners claim their medicines can reduce the debilitating illnesses associated with HIV/AIDS, though more research and testing is required before this can be accepted as a scientific fact.

Yoga

Unlike Ayurveda and Siddha, yoga does not offer any drugs; it is nevertheless a holistic system that promotes healthy living. Through a combination of bodily postures, breathing exercises and meditation, it attempts to achieve a perfect balance between the body and the mind, which can unite the individual with the divine.

Yoga originated in the ancient Vedic period but was given a formal structure by the sage Patanjali, called the 'Father of Yoga', in the *Yoga Sutra*, a book of 195 aphorisms, in c. 200 BC. At the heart of his philosophy was the eightfold yogic path (ashtanga yoga) for all-round development leading to the ultimate goal of the union of the individual soul with the Universal Spirit. The eightfold path, known as the eight limbs of Patanjali, are: *yama* (abstentions)—non-violence, truth, abstention from theft, continence, abstention from possessions; *niyama* (observances)—purity, contentment, austerity, self-study and living with an awareness of the divine; asana (postures); *pratyahara* (sense control); *pranayama* (breath control); *dharana* (concentration); *dhyana* (meditation) and *samadhi* (absolute bliss). The eight work together to increase concentration and mental purity and rejuvenate the different organs in the body to promote vitality, vigour and longevity.

According to the philosophy of yoga, most diseases, whether they are mental, psychosomatic or physical, originate in the mind through faulty thinking, living and eating. The aim of yoga, therefore, is to correct these negative habits. Like Ayurveda, it advocates cleansing the body as the first step in curing any ailment. Yoga does not use any drugs but helps to develop full efficiency of the various organs of the body, particularly the excretory and urinary systems through which all the harmful toxins are eliminated.

Today, particularly in the Western countries where it is widely popular, yoga is synonymous with Hatha Yoga, a system introduced by Yogi Swatmarama, a 15th-century sage. It differs from Patanjali's yoga in that it focuses on the purification of the physical being leading to the purification of the mind. (Patanjali's yoga begins with the purity of the mind and spirit before going on to the body.) Hatha Yoga offers a variety of postures for meditation and to cure health problems, strengthen the back and improve digestion. It is seen as an effective means to physical health, vitality and spiritual mastery.

IMPORTANT OF BREATHING RIGHT

According to yogic principles, pranayama is essential for general health and to control the vital life energy. Oxygen is believed to be the most vital nutrient for the body, particularly the brain, which requires it more than any other organ. Negative thoughts, depression and mental sluggishness can occur when the brain does not get enough oxygen. Breathing itself has four stages: inhalation, pause, exhalation and pause again; in yoga, the pauses are prolonged to benefit the body and state of mind.

THE INDIAN
CALENDAR

INDIAN NATIONAL CALENDAR

There are several calendars in use in India, the earliest dating back to the Hindu calendar used in ancient Vedic times. However, the Indian government has officially adopted the Indian National Calendar for civilian use in the country and the Gregorian calendar for administrative purposes. The Indian National Calendar is a modified version of the traditional calendars used by Hindus.

The Hindu calendar system was introduced in the Jyotish Vedanga, the section of the *Vedas* that deals with astronomy and astrology. It was standardised in the *Surya Siddhanta*, an astronomical treatise written between the 3rd and 4th centuries, and subsequently reformed by astronomers such as Aryabhata in the 5th century and Bhaskara in the 12th century. According to the ancient calendar system, the calendrical day starts with local sunrise. It has five properties: *tithi*, *vaasara*, *nakshatra*, *yoga* and *karana*. *Tithi* is the lunar day, calculated from the angular difference between the sun and the moon; *vaasara* or *vaara* refers to the seven days of the week; the ecliptic or path of the sun through the sky is divided into 27 *nakshatra* or lunar mansions, similar to zodiac constellations; *yoga* is calculated from adding the longitude of the sun and the moon and dividing the sum by 27; and *karana* is half of the *tithi*.

In ancient India, the length of the year ranged from 365.258681 days to 365.258756 days, compared with the modern length of 365.25636 days; the old values are still in use in many traditional Indian calendars. The traditional calendar plays a key role in the lives of Hindus. It is referred to constantly by priests and religious leaders to calculate the dates of festivals as well as auspicious days and times for important events such as marriages, launching a new business venture and performing religious rituals. Both solar and lunar movements are used in the calculation of dates.

To bring about uniformity in the use of calendars in India, a reform exercise was undertaken in the 1950s. Many different calendars based on the movements of the sun and moon were in use then, and different assumptions about the length of months and years brought about variations among them.

The Indian National Calendar takes off from the Saka Era. The first year is counted from the first year of the Saka Era in 78. Therefore, 2006 in the Gregorian calendar translates to 1927–1928 in the Saka Era. This calendar, with a normal year of 365 days, was adopted by the Indian government on 22 March 1957 along with the Gregorian calendar. The Gregorian calendar is used for official purposes such as news broadcasts by the state-owned radio network, All India Radio, calendars issued by the Indian government and government communications meant for the public.

The first day of the Indian National Calendar coincides with 22 March in the Gregorian calendar, except in a leap year when it starts on 21 March. The months have a fixed number of days, either 30 or 31. The five months from the second to the sixth have mean lengths over 30.5 days and their lengths are rounded up to 31 days. The remaining months have 30 days.

INDIAN NATIONAL CALENDAR

Month	Number of Days	Start date according to Gregorian Calendar
Chaitra	30 (31 in leap year)	22 March (21 March in leap year)
Vaisakha	31	21 April
Jyaistha	31	22 May
Asadha	31	22 June
Sravana	31	23 July
Bhadra	31	23 August
Asvina	30	23 September
Kartika	30	23 October
Agrahayana	30	22 November
Pausa	30	22 December
Magha	30	21 January
Phalguna	30	20 February

INDIAN FESTIVALS

India's rich cultural and religious heritage and its multitude of gods and goddesses have laid the foundation for a festive calendar year replete with celebrations of all kinds. Some festivals such as Diwali, Holi, Raksha Bandhan, Id-ul-Zuha, Id-ul-Fitr and Christmas are celebrated at a national level; others are particular to a region, a state or a certain tribe. Hindus also dedicate special days for each one of their numerous deities, celebrating their birthdays, marriages and even their victory over an evil demon. In Bihar state, for instance, Chatt Puja, a popular festival devoted to the Sun God, is celebrated twice a year. There are also festivities to mark the start of the harvest season and the new year, which differ from region to region.

The harvest festival of Onam is specific to the southern state of Kerala, while Ugadi, the Telugu New Year, is celebrated in neighbouring Karnataka. With the Indian calendar dependent on the lunar and solar cycles, there are no fixed dates for the various festivals, though they usually fall in the same month or period of the year.

Diwali, Festival of Lights

Diwali, or Deepavali, is the biggest festival in the Indian calendar, and is celebrated with much fanfare in all the regions of the country where Hindus reside. It is also an important date for members of the Jain and Sikh communities.

The festival gets its name from the Sanskrit word *dipavali* meaning 'row of lights'. On this day, people light up their homes with earthen lamps (*diyas*), candles, electric lights and firecrackers to express their joy and mood of celebration. Days preceding the festival are marked by spring cleaning, and decoration with *rangoli* to prepare the home for the goddess Lakshmi. Sweetmeats are also prepared or bought and distributed among family and friends in the general spirit of bonhomie. Diwali is also a time to wear new clothes, new jewellery and give gifts to near and dear ones.

The festival has its origins in a number of legends, the most popular being the story of Lord Rama from the Hindu epic *Ramayana*. According to one legend, Diwali commemorates the slaughter of the evil king of Pragjyotishpur by Lord Krishna. The evil king had kidnapped 16,000 daughters of the gods and stolen the earrings of Aditi, mother of the gods. The gods asked Krishna for help. After a mighty battle, he succeeded in killing the demon, freeing the girls and recovering the earrings. The victorious Krishna returned home and was bathed with scented oils, giving rise to the practice of having an oil bath on Diwali day in some parts of the country.

The festival is observed for five continuous days and usually takes place in the months of October/November. The first day of the festival is Dhanteras, and Hindus believe it is an auspicious day to buy gold, silver or some metal object for the home; the second day is Narka Chaturdashi or Choti Diwali and the third day is the actual Diwali, a new moon day and the most auspicious of the festival. It is the day of Lakshmi Puja, when Hindus pray to the goddess Lakshmi and light up their homes to welcome her. She is believed to enter the home and shower wealth and prosperity on the inhabitants. In the states of Bengal and Bihar, the people pray to the goddess Kali on Diwali, not Lakshmi. Some people also gamble on Diwali—according to a Shiva-Parvati legend, anyone who gambles on Diwali will prosper all year. The fourth day of the festival is known as Padwa or Varshapratipada. It marks the coronation of the legendary King Vikramaditya, as well as the start of the new year in the Hindu calendar. Hindus thus consider this day as an auspicious time to start a new venture. The fifth day is known as Bhaiya Duj in the Hindi-speaking belt and Bhau Beej in the Marathi-speaking community, and it celebrates the relationship between brothers and sisters.

WHAT DIWALI MEANS TO SIKHS AND JAINS

Diwali is an important festival in Sikhism. Sikhs celebrate it for two reasons—to mark the release from prison of their sixth guru, Hargobind Singh, in 1619, and to mark the day the foundation stone of the holiest Sikh shrine, the Golden Temple at Amritsar, was laid in 1588. Jains celebrate Diwali because it was the day Jainism founder Lord Mahavira, attained *moksha* (freedom or salvation from the cycle of birth and death).

Dussehra

Celebrated in a variety of ways across the country, Dussehra is an important Hindu festival that symbolises the triumph of good over evil. This day marks the destruction of Ravana, demon king of Lanka, at the hands of Lord Rama (an incarnation of Vishnu). As related in the *Ramayana*, the war against Ravana lasted for ten days, with Rama finally vanquishing the demon on the tenth day. During the nine preceding days, Rama is said to have prayed to the mother goddess, Durga, for strength and success in battle.

Dussehra falls in the month of October every year at the end of the nine-day Navratri Festival (or Durga Puja in Bengal). The story of Rama and Ravana, known as Ram Leela, is enacted in dramas in cities, towns and villages across the country during the nine days of Navratri.

On Dussehra day, effigies of Ravana, his brother Kumbhakaran and son Meghnad are stuffed with firecrackers and set alight at sunset, as crowds gather to celebrate the victory of good over evil. In Bengal, the occasion is celebrated as the day Durga killed the terrible demon Mahishasur. In some homes on this day, all kinds of weapons, tools, instruments, pens and pencils are worshipped, because they are symbols of the means to fight injustice and evil, and are placed in front of the gods. In the army, police and paramilitary organisations, all vehicles are cleaned thoroughly and prayers are offered. Like other Indian festivals, this is also a day of family get-togethers and feasting.

In Bengal, where Durga Puja is the most important Hindu festival, temporary structures with large images of Durga, known as *pandals*, are set up for public veneration of the goddess. Community members get together every day during the festive period to celebrate with song and dance performances and feasting. In Kolkata, capital of Bengal, thousands of *pandals* are erected and people are known to go *pandal*-hopping in the carnival-like atmosphere, in a spirit of joy and celebration. On the 10th day of the festival—Dussehra day—huge images of Durga are carried through the streets in a procession and immersed in a nearby body of water.

Holi, Festival of Colours

Holi falls on the day after the first full moon in the month of March. It is a festival marked by colour, exuberance, joyous dance and play, as people get together to celebrate the end of winter and the start of the spring season. Holi has taken on a somewhat wild and riotous character in recent times, with participants throwing water balloons, squirting coloured water with water guns and even using buckets of water to drench others, in addition to smearing the traditional coloured powder (*gulal*) on each other. *Thandai* is a popular milk-based drink which is a favourite of revellers during the Holi festival, while the intoxicant *bhang* is consumed by the more adventurous.

A number of legends surround the festival of Holi and its origins. One revolves around the kingdom of the mythological King Hiranyakashipu, his sister Holika and his son Prahlad. Holika is said to have died in a fire while protecting Prahlad from the wrath of his father, who had declared himself as god. Prahlad, a devotee of Vishnu, remained unscathed in the fire. Holi is named after Holika, and her effigy is burnt in a bonfire on the eve of the festival in some parts of India. Another legend revolves around Shiva and Kama, the God of Love. Shiva is said to have burnt Kama for disturbing his meditation, hence the bonfire on the eve of Holi.

In the cities of Vrindavan and Mathura, in Uttar Pradesh state, Holi is associated with Hindu god Krishna and his companion, Radha. In this region, the birthplace of Krishna, Holi is celebrated over 16 days with colourful processions, folk songs and dances. Songs and dances also mark the festival of colours in the rural parts of Maharashtra state, where it is known as Rangapanchami. In Jaisalmer, Rajasthan, the Mandir Palace is a favourite spot for celebratory dances and folk songs amidst the profusion of coloured powder.

Raksha Bandhan

Popularly known as Rakhi, this Hindu festival falls in the month of August on full moon day. Traditionally, it commemorates the bond between a brother and sister, with the brother pledging love and protection for his sister. Unlike other Indian festivals, a simple ritual is performed to mark Raksha Bandhan, which literally means 'ties of protection'. A sister applies a *tikka*, a red vermillion dot, on her brother's forehead, says a small prayer for his health and well-being, then ties the *rakhi* on his wrist. The *rakhi* can take any form, from a simple thread to a more elaborate bunch of colourful strings decorated with stones and attractive motifs. She completes the ceremony by offering him some sweets. He in turn promises to love and protect his sister and gives her a gift, commonly of cash, as a token of his affection.

This festival has been given a broader interpretation with the sibling relationship extended to include ties between two friends who are like brother and sister, or even between a leader and his subordinate. Priests have been known to tie *rakhis* on members of their congregation, women tie *rakhis* on soldiers to wish them well on the field and members of the public congregate to tie the thread on local leaders and even the prime minister of India.

This festival, too, has its origins in Hindu mythology. According to one legend, Sachi, the wife of Sun God Indra, tied a thread around her husband's wrist to ensure his victory in a duel with demon Vritra. Another legend from the *Mahabharata* revolves around Draupadi, the wife of the Pandavas and of Hindu god Krishna. Draupadi is said to have torn a strip of silk off her sari and tied it around Krishna's wrist to stem the flow of blood after he suffered an injury in battle. Krishna promised to repay her for her concern. He was able to do so years later, when Draupadi was about to be disrobed by her brother-in-law, Duryodhana. Krishna came to her aid and ensured that her sari could not be taken off.

EXCHANGE OF RAKHIS AMONG ROYALTY

Historical records reveal countless instances of exchanges of *rakhis* among members of royalty. In one example from the 16th century, Queen Karnawati, anxious about an imminent invasion of her kingdom Chittor by Bahadur Shah of Mewar, sent a *rakhi* to Mughal Emperor Humayun. He accepted her as a 'sister' and immediately came to her rescue.

Baisakhi

Baisakhi, or Vaisakhi, is a north Indian harvest festival with a special significance for the Sikhs, for it marks their New Year and the founding of the Sikh Khalsa. The Khalsa (The Pure Ones) is a brotherhood of Sikhs who have taken a vow to uphold the principles laid down by the 10th guru, Guru Gobind Singh. This is one of the few Hindu festivals that has a fixed date, falling on 13 April every year at the start of the solar calendar.

It was on Baisakhi day in 1699 that Guru Gobind Singh founded the Khalsa with the initiation of the Panj Piare, or Beloved Five, giving Sikhs an identity and a code of conduct to live by. The initiation ceremony took place in a tent. The guru, holding a sword in his hand, asked for volunteers who would be prepared to give up their lives if required. One by one, he led five men into a tent and, after the initiation ceremony with a sword, sprinkled holy water (*amrit*) on them and called them the Beloved Five. These men were to dedicate themselves to the service of others and to the pursuit of justice. They were required to wear the five symbols of their new identity: uncut hair, a comb in the hair, a steel bracelet, a sword and shorts.

The Sikhs celebrate Baisakhi by thronging Sikh temples, known as *gurudwaras*, where they pray and make offerings. Processions of Sikh devotees who sing folk songs and perform the energetic Bhangra dance are also common.

Buddha Poornima Or Buddha Jayanti

Vesak, which falls between April and May, is celebrated as Buddha Poornima or Buddha Jayanti in India. It is the most important day for Buddhists because it commemorates the birth, enlightenment and death of the Buddha.

To participate in the Buddha Poornima celebrations, Buddhists from all over the world congregate at Bodh Gaya in the Indian state of Bihar, where Siddhartha Gautama achieved enlightenment under a bodhi tree. The celebrations include prayer meetings, religious discourses, recitation of Buddhist scriptures and meditation. The Mahabodhi Temple complex in Bodh Gaya, which houses all the sacred spots where the Buddha meditated after his enlightenment, is decorated with colourful flags and flowers as part of the celebrations. Pilgrims pray at the *bodhi* tree, which has been replanted many times in the 2,500 years since Siddhartha Gautama attained enlightenment under it. Under the tree lies the rectangular slab of sandstone known as the *vajrasana*, or diamond throne, placed at the exact spot the Buddha is believed to have attained enlightenment.

Other important centres in India where Buddhist pilgrims congregate for Buddha Poornima celebrations include Sarnath, where the Buddha gave his first sermon, and Kushinagar, in Uttar Pradesh state, where he died in c. 486 BC.

Mahavira Jayanti

Mahavira Jayanti is the birth anniversary of Lord Mahavira, the founder of modern Jainism, and is celebrated in March or April by Jains everywhere; it is observed with particular fervour in the states of Rajasthan and Gujarat, where large numbers of Jains reside.

Grand chariot processions with the images of Mahavira, temple ceremonies and the reading of Jain scriptures are some of the ways in which Jains celebrate the festival at pilgrimage spots such as Girnar and Palitana in Gujarat, Mahavirji in Rajasthan and Vaishali, the birthplace of Mahavira in Bihar state. Palitana has over 1,000 Jain shrines and 800 temples and is considered one of the most important pilgrimage spots for Jains.

Navroz

Navroz, which means 'new day', marks the start of the new year for the Zoroastrian Parsi community. It coincides with the spring equinox and is a time for wearing new clothes, feasting and exchanging gifts and greetings with friends and family. According to popular legend, Navroz, or Jamshed-e-Navroz as it is also called, is named after the mythical Persian King Jamshed. He was the first to celebrate the festival to mark the change of seasons from winter to summer.

People visit fire temples on this day. At home, they prepare a special Navroz table that is covered with a white cloth and holds a number of items, each with a special significance. These include a copy of their scriptures, the Gathas; a lit lamp; a bowl of water with live fish; an earthenware plate with sprouted wheat or beans to signify prosperity; flowers; a silver coin to symbolise wealth; painted eggs for productivity; and sweets and rosewater for happiness.

The table also holds seven foods beginning with 'sh' in Persian: *sharab* (wine), *shakar* (sugar), *shir* (milk), *shirinberenj* (sweetmeat), *shirin* (sweet), *shira* (syrup) and *shahad* (honey). There are also seven things that start with 's': *sirocco* (vinegar), *samna* (sumac), *seibu* (apple), *sir* (garlic), *senjed* (sorb tree berry) and *sabzi* (green vegetables). Fruits, dried fruits, nuts and pumpkin seeds symbolising creation complete the spread. Visitors on Navroz day are first taken to the Navroz table where certain rituals are performed, after which they are taken to another table where a meal has been laid out for them.

RITUALS ON NAVROZ

On Navroz, it is customary for the woman of the house to first make visitors smile into a mirror to ensure they smile throughout the year. She then asks them to look at a silver coin, so that they may have wealth all year round, and sprinkles rosewater on their hands for good health.

THE RESURGENCE
OF INDIA

INDIA IN THE 21ST CENTURY

India in the 21st century is a country on a roll, powered by an economy in overdrive. The transformation of India from an underdeveloped, overpopulated country deep in the throes of an economic crisis in 1991, to one of the fastest growing economies in the world, has been truly remarkable. Today, the country is the outsourcing centre of the world, renowned for its knowledge-based industries and its software and information technology specialists.

The profound change and impressive growth is a direct result of reform measures taken by Indian leaders, particularly Prime Minister Narasimha Rao in 1991, to open up an economy shackled by corruption and the inefficiency of state-owned enterprises—a result, some say, of Nehru's economic policies. Liberalisation of the economy has allowed India to integrate with the global economy and helped push economic growth to record highs in the 1990s. This trend has continued in the 21st century, driving India to the centre stage in Asia, as well as in the global arena. However, poor infrastructure, gross overpopulation, poverty (29 per cent of the people live below the poverty line), illiteracy and a looming AIDS crisis are among the major challenges facing the world's largest democracy as it moves steadily forward, alongside China, on the high road to becoming an Asian superpower.

Congress Politics

While India has made rapid and radical strides in economic growth, its political landscape has maintained a certain continuity, except for minor deviations, in the form of the almost unbroken domination of the Congress Party, which has governed the country for as many as 44 of the 59 years since independence in 1947— excluding the years since 2004 that it has led a coalition government in Delhi. And for at least 37 of these years, the prime minister has hailed from the Nehru-Gandhi family. The ruling partiesand coalition alliances have largely maintained the secular and democratic framework of this multi-religious and multi-ethnic country.

The dynastic rule begun by Jawaharlal Nehru when he became the first prime minister in 1947 continued with his daughter, Indira Gandhi, and Indira's elder son, Rajiv Gandhi. (The name Gandhi comes from Indira's husband, Feroze Gandhi; she is not related to Mahatma Gandhi.) Rajiv's widow, Sonia, has been president of the Congress Party since April 1998 and is responsible for reviving the party, out of power since 1996, and helping it emerge victorious in the December 2003 elections with its coalition partners.

Except for a stint when Lal Bahadur Shashtri became prime minister after Nehru's death in 1964, Indira Gandhi governed India for a greater part of the 1960s and 1970s and continued some of her father's policies. Indira, expected to be a submissive leader who could be dominated by the Congress, proved to be a strong and politically astute prime minister who managed to consolidate her power within the party ranks and surrounded herself with a coterie of loyalists. She centralised power in her own hands and crushed any dissension in the party. It was her insecurity and the perceived threat to her power that led her to take the unprecedented step of declaring an Emergency in India in June 1975. This allowed her to arrest her main opponents and take control of the press, upturning the primary pillars of democracy that were so dear to her father's heart. Indira lifted the Emergency in January 1977 and scheduled parliamentary elections, confident she would be victorious. However, the electorate, still smarting from the excesses of the authoritarian Emergency rule, voted her out of power, choosing to reject the Congress for the first time since independence.

Opposition in Power

A coalition government led by the centrist Janata Party brought winds of change into government after three decades of Congress rule, but the new leaders also brought with them petty party politics and dissensions in the ranks of the coalition partners. The government, first led by 81-year-old veteran politician Morarji Desai, and later by Charan Singh, lasted for three years until it lost a majority in the Lok Sabha (Lower House of Parliament) and had to resign. In the 1980 elections, Indira Gandhi made a comeback and stayed in power until her assassination by her Sikh security guards on 31 October 1984. Her son, Rajiv, an airline pilot who had spent just four years in politics, became the Congress Party president and the new prime minister of India, perpetuating the Nehru-Gandhi dynastic rule. Indira's younger son, Sanjay, who was a member of parliament and widely believed to be her political heir, died in a plane crash in June 1980.

The Opposition parties, lacking a big enough following among the Indian masses, have made consistent bids for government since their first taste of power in the 1970s, but they have not been able to cobble together a strong and united force to unseat the age-old Congress party and sustain their rule. In December 1989, they banded to form the National Front, which did succeed in winning the elections but only lasted for two years until 1991, when Congress came back in power. Rajiv Gandhi, slated to become prime minister, was assassinated by supporters of the Sri Lankan LTTE on 21 May 1991, during the electoral process. With his widow, Italian-born Sonia, showing no interest in politics, the Congress selected P V Narasimha Rao as prime minister, the first politician outside the Nehru-Gandhi dynasty to lead the country in government since Lal Bahadur Shastri in 1966.

Hindu Nationalists to the Fore

The 1991 election marked the emergence of the right-wing Bharatiya Janata Party (BJP) to national-level politics. The party doubled its share of the vote to 20 per cent and became the second largest party in Parliament. Its growing popularity was fuelled by Hindu nationalist feeling over the Ayodhya site claimed by both Hindus and Muslims as sacred. The Ayodhya issue was ignited by BJP leader Lal Krishna Advani, who set off on a *rath yatra*, or chariot procession, across north India in September 1990. He called on Hindus to tear down the existing Babri Masjid mosque in Ayodhya and restore the Hindu Rama temple destroyed by Muslim invader Mahmud of Ghazni at the same site in the 10th century. Advani's call to rally Hindus on the Ayodhya issue was a political strategy that served the BJP well. Two years later, on 6 December 1992, Hindu radicals from all over India tore down the Babri Masjid. This set off massive communal riots, killing thousands of people. Top BJP leaders were arrested for inciting the destruction of the mosque.

The BJP increased its share of parliamentary seats in the 1998 election and came to power with its allies in a coalition government—now the norm in politically fragmented India, where it is no longer possible for a single party to muster enough votes to secure a majority on its own. Charismatic BJP leader Atal Behari Vajpayee, as prime minister, led the 18-party National Democratic Alliance in the new government. Vajpayee's government led the country into the 21st century to achieve high economic growth and a stronger position in the international arena during its rule. Confident about its standing with the Indian electorate and armed with its 'India Shining' advertising campaign highlighting its accomplishments, the BJP called for elections in April/May 2004. Party leaders, in a buoyant mood, had no doubt they would be voted back to power. Instead, to the astonishment of BJP politicians and members of the urban electorate, the party suffered an unexpected defeat. The Congress Party-led coalition, with support coming from the marginalised grassroots electorate, formed the new government with Dr Manmohan Singh as prime minister.

Foreign Relations

India's exceptional growth in the software and IT-enabled services sector has helped it play a greater role in global business, which in turn has enabled it to forge closer economic and diplomatic ties with other countries. A case in point is the United States. India, as a non-aligned nation, has traditionally been wary of aligning itself with any power bloc, but since 1998, when US President Bill Clinton attempted to cement ties with India after its nuclear tests, the two countries have drawn closer. India has also warmed up towards China, underscored by an expansion in two-way trade, which has nearly doubled from 2001 to 2004.

India's relations with its neighbour Pakistan have been turbulent in the decades since independence, with the two nations having gone to war several times over the thorny issue of Kashmir. India has voiced concerns about what it claims are Pakistan-sponsored terrorist strikes on its territory, with one of the most virulent being an attack on the Indian Parliament on 13 December 2001. The two sides have been holding foreign secretary-level talks as part of their ongoing peace process without making much headway. Indian Prime Minister Manmohan Singh and Pakistani Prime Minister Pervez Musharraf met on the sidelines of the Non-Aligned Summit in Havana, Cuba, in September 2006 and agreed to create a joint anti-terrorist mechanism to tackle the problem.

Continuity and Change

India presents an intriguing paradox of continuity and change as it forges ahead. Even while it rapidly transforms itself into an IT powerhouse of the 21st century, it remains steeped in culture and tradition, a land of snake charmers and folklore, the vigorous Bhangra dance and colourful *batik*. Its multilinguistic, multi-ethnic and multi-religious society, an outcome of its complex origins thousands of years ago, has given India a fascinating diversity. A country of over one billion people, it is more like a continent straddling the mighty Himalayas on one side and the Deccan Plateau on the other. India's borders have changed countless times in its tumultuous history—from the ancient period when its territory covered parts of Afghanistan, Burma, Nepal, Pakistan and Bangladesh, to the present day when it is the seventh largest country in the world, with these same nations as its neighbours.

India's multiplicity extends to its languages, religions, arts, crafts, cuisine and music, which differ from one state to another and from one region to the next. It is this rich cultural mosaic that continues to give India its identity and singularity.

B I B L I O G R A P H Y

Alyssa, A., & Oldenburg, P. (2005) *India Briefing: Takeoff at Last*. Armonk,
     NY: M.E. Sharpe

Ancient India. (1996). In *World Civilizations*. Retrieved 12 Nov 2006 from
     Washington State University website: http://www.wsu.edu/~dee/
     ANCINDIA/GUPTA.HTM

Ayurveda. (n.d.) In Ayurvedic Foundations Online. Retrieved 27 Nov
     2006 from Ayurvedic Foundations website: http://www.ayur.com/about.
     html.

Ayurveda. (n.d.) In National Center for Complementary and Alternative
     Medicine (NCCAM) Online. Retrieved 27 Nov 2006 from NCCAM
     website: http://nccam.nih.gov/health/ayurveda/

BBC. (2006) S Asia rivals continue key talks. Retrieved 23 Nov 2006
     from bbc.co.uk. website: http://news.bbc.co.uk/1/hi/world/south_
     asia/6144360.stm

Brahmi Script. (n.d.) In Central Institute of Indian Languages Website.
     Retrieved 2 Dec 2006 from: http://www.ciil.org/Main/Programmes/
     LIPIKA/brahmi.htm

Census India. (2001) Retrieved 12 Dec 2006 from http://www.
     censusindia.net/religiondata/Summary%20Buddhists.pdf

Centres of Buddhist Art. (n.d.) In Crafts of India. Retrieved 3 Dec 2006
     from Crafts of India website: http://www.craftsinindia.com/indian-art-
     culture/centers-of-buddhist-art.html

Chaudhari, A. (2004) *The Vintage Book of Modern Indian Literature*. New York: Vintage Books

Delhi Sultanate. (n.d.) In HighBeam Encyclopedia. Retrieved 15 Nov 2006 from HighBeam Encyclopedia website: http://www.encyclopedia.com/doc/1E1- DelhiSul.html

Department of Ancient Near Eastern Art. (2000) In Timeline of Art History. Retrieved 19 Nov 2006 from the The Metropolitan Museum of Art website: http://www.metmuseum.org/toah/hd/silk/hd_silk.htm (October 2000)

Diwali. (2006). In Encyclopædia Britannica. Retrieved 30 Oct 2006, from Encyclopædia Britannica Online: http://www.britannica.com/eb/article-9030695

Dravidian Languages. (n.d.) In Columbia Encyclopedia Sixth Edition. Retrieved 2 Dec 2006 from Bartleby.com: http://www.bartleby.com/65/dr/Dravidia-l.html

Fallon, S. (1998) *A Dictionary of Hindustani Proverbs*. New Delhi: Asian Educational Services

Ganeri, A. (1994). *Exploration Into India*. London: Belitha Press

Ganti, T. (2004). *Bollywood a guidebook to popular Hindi cinema*. London: Routledge

Gray, D. (n.d.) Indic Mathematics: India and the Scientific Revolution. Retrieved 24 Nov 2006 from Infinity Foundation website: http://www.infinityfoundation.com/ECITmathframeset.html

Gupta India. (n.d.). In World Civilizations. Retrieved 12 Nov 2006 from Shannon Duffy home page in Loyola University, New Orleans website: http://www.loyno.edu/~seduffy/guptaindia.html

Gupta Period. (n.d.). In WebIndia123.com. Retrieved 12 Nov 2006 from WebIndia123.com website: http://www.webindia123.com/history/ANCIENT/gupta_period.htm

Harsha. (n.d.). In IndiaandIndians.com. Retrieved 13 Nov 2006 from India and Indians.com website: http://www.indiaandindians.com/india_history/harsha.php

Hatha Yoga. (n.d.) In Yoga Guide Online. Retrieved 27 Nov 2006 from Yoga Guide website: http://yoga-guideto.com/a/183325/Hatha+yoga.html

Hinduism. (2006) In BBC. Retrieved 31 Oct 2006 from bbc.co.uk: http://www.bbc.co.uk/religion/religious/hinduism/deities/; http://www.bbc.co.uk/religion/religious/hinduism/holydays/diwali.shtml

Henderson, C. (2002) *Culture and Customs of India*. Westport, Conn.; London: Greenwood

Hindi History (2006). In Hindi Society Singapore. Retrieved 29 Oct 2006 from Hindi Society, Singapore website: http://www.hindisociety.com/ArticleHindiHistory.htm

Husain, S.A. (2005) The National Culture of India. New Delhi: National Book Trust

India 2006 *A Reference Manual*. (2006) New Delhi: Publications Division

India. (2006) In CIA Factbook. Retrieved 7 Nov 2006 from CIA Factbook website: http://www.cia.gov/cia/publications/factbook/fields/2075.html

India. (2006). In Encyclopaedia Britannica. Retrieved 20 Oct 2006 from Encyclopaedia Britannica Online: http://www.britannica.com/eb/article-9111197; Retrieved 10 Nov 2006, from http://www.britannica.com/eb/article-46865; Retrieved 13 Nov 2006 from http://www.britannica.com/eb/article-46889

India. (2006). In Encyclopædia Britannica. Retrieved 21 Nov 2006, from Encyclopædia Britannica Online: http://www.britannica.com/eb/article-47052

India. (2006) In Ministry of Home Affairs, Government of India. Retrieved 12 Nov 2006 from Ministry of Home Affairs, Government of India website: http://mha.nic.in/his1.htm

India. (n.d.) In Columbia Encyclopedia Sixth Edition. Retrieved 20 Nov 2006 from Bartleby.com website: http://www.bartleby.com/65/in/IndianMu.html

India (2006) In World Bank Online. Retrieved 23 Nov 2006 from World Bank website.: http://devdata.worldbank.org/AAG/ind_aag.pdf

India Becomes a Republic. (n.d.) In BBC Online. Retrieved 22 Nov 2006 from bbc.co.uk website: http://news.bbc.co.uk/onthisday/hi/dates/stories/january/26/newsid_3475000/3475 569.stm

Indian Literature. (n.d.) In Columbia Electronic Encyclopedia. Retrieved 28 Nov 2006 from Columbia The Free Dictionary website: http://columbia.thefreedictionary.com/Indian+literature

Indian Temples. (n.d.) In TempleNet Online. Retrieved 12 Dec 2006 from TempleNet website: http://www.indiantemples.com/arch.html

Indo-Scythians. (n.d.). In Wikipedia, the free encyclopedia. Retrieved 9 Nov 2006 from Reference.com website: http://www.reference.com/browse/wiki/Indo-Scythians.

Jainism. (2006). In BBC. Retrieved 31 Oct 2006 from bbc.co.uk: http://www.bbc.co.uk/religion/religious/jainism/living

Jamanadas, K. (2000) Rajput Period was Dark Age of India. Retrieved 14 Nov2006 from www.ambedkar.org website: http://www.ambedkar.org/jamanadas/RajputPeriod.htm

Jataka Tales. (1995) In Pravardigar Press. Retrieved 30 Nov 2006 from Pravardigar Press website: http://www.parvardigarpress.com/jataka.html

Jataka Tales. (n.d.) In Jatak Katha. Retrieved 30 Nov 2006 from Jatak Katha: A Collection of Buddhist Tales website: http://www.jatakkatha.com/

Jhaveri, A. (2005). *A Guide to 101 Modern and Contemporary Indian Artists*. Mumbai: India Book House

Kiran Desai. (2006) In Booker Prize Online. Retrieved 29 Nov 2006 from Booker Prize website: http://www.themanbookerprize.com/pressoffice/release.php?r=28#titletop

Kishore, P. & Ganpati, A.K. (2003). *India: An Illustrated History*. New York: Hippocrene Books

Lodha, R. & Bagga. A. (2000) Tradional Indian Systems of Medicine. In Annals of the Academy of Medicine, Singapore. Jan; 29(1):37-41

Mahatma Gandhi. (n.d.) In Indian National Congress Online. Retrieved 21 Nov 2006 from Indian National Congress website: http://aicc.org.in/mahatma_gandhi.php

Majestic Taj. (n.d.) In Incredible India. Retrieved 3 Dec 2006 from Incredible India website: http://www.incredibleindia.org/newsite/cms_page.asp?pageid=2740

Mcleod, J. (2002) *The History of India*. Westport CT: Greenwood Press

Mehrgarh. (n.d.). Wikipedia. Retrieved 30 Nov 2006, from Answers.com Web site: http://www.answers.com/topic/mehrgarh

Metcalf, B. & Metcalf, T. (2002). *A Concise History of India*. New York : Cambridge University Press

Ministry of Information and Broadcasting,India (2006) *India 2006: A Reference Manual*. New Delhi: Publications Division

Mishra, V. (2002). *Bollywood Cinema Temples of Desire*. London: Routledge

Mughals. (1999) In World Civilisations, Washington State University.

Retrieved 17 Nov 2006 from Washington State University website:
http://www.wsu.edu:8080/~dee/MUGHAL/ORIGIN.HTM

Munshi Premchand: The Great Novelist. (n.d.) In Press Information Bureau
(PIB), Government of India. Retrieved 29 Nov 2006 from PIB website:
http://pib.nic.in/feature/feyr2001/fjul2001/f190720011.html

O'Brien, D. (2006) *The Penguin India Reference Yearbook 2006*. New Delhi:
Penguin Books India

Patanjali Yoga. (n.d.) In Global Oneness Foundation Online. Retrieved
27 Nov 2006 from Global Oneness Foundation website: http://www.
experiencefestival.com/a/Patanjali_Yoga/id/22018

Puranas. (n.d.) In Manas Online. Retrieved 29 Nov 2006 from Manas
website: http://www.sscnet.ucla.edu/southasia/Religions/texts/Puranas.
html

Rabindranath Tagore. (n.d.) From Nobel Lectures, Literature 1901–1967,
Editor Horst Frenz, Elsevier Publishing Company, Amsterdam, 1969.
Retrieved 29 Nov 2006 from http://nobelprize.org/nobel_prizes/
literature/laureates/1913/tagore-bio.html

Rani Jhansi. (n.d.) In National Informatics Centre (NIC), Jhansi website.
Retrieved 6 Dec 2006 from NIC website: http://jhansi.nic.in/rani.htm

Roberts, S. (n.d.) Patanjali and his eight-fold path of yoga. Retrieved 27
Nov 2006 from Yoga Movement website: http://www.yogamovement.
com/resources/patanjali.html

Rosenberg, D. (1997) *Folklore, Myths, and Legends: A World Perspective*.
Lincolnwood, Illinois: NTC Publishing Group

Salt March to Dandi. (n.d) In Emory University Online. Retrieved 21 Nov
2006 from Emory University website: http://www.english.emory.edu/
Bahri/Dandi.html

Samudragupta. (n.d). In AllExperts Enclyclopedia. Retrieved 12 Nov 2006 from AllExperts website: http://experts.about.com/e/s/sa/ samudragupta.htm

Sanskrit. (n.d.). The Columbia Electronic Encyclopedia, Sixth Edition. Retrieved 6 Dec 2006, from Answers.com website: http://www. answers.com/topic/sanskrit

Sarnath. (n.d.) In HighBeam Encyclopedia. Retrieved 5 Nov 2006, from HighBeam Encyclopedia Online: http://www.encyclopedia.com/ doc/1E1-Sarnath.html

Shankracharya, (n.d.). In Poet Seers. Retrieved 14 Nov 2006 from Poet Seers website: http://www.poetseers.org/spiritual_and_devotional_ poets/india/shankar/

Sivaramamurti, C. (2002) *Indian Painting*. New Delhi: National Book Trust

Srinivasan, R. (1999) *Facets of Indian Culture*. Mumbai: Bharatiya Vidya Bhavan

Stein, B. (1998). *A History of India*. Oxford: Blackwell Publishers

Stone Age Man Lived in These Rock Shelters (30 June 2002), The Tribune, Retrieved 30 Nov 2006 from The Tribune website: http://www. tribuneindia.com/2002/20020630/spectrum/travel.htm

Sunga Dynasty. (2006). In Britannica Concise Encyclopaedia. Retrieved 10 Nov 2006, from Encyclopaedia Britannica Online: http://geoanalyzer. britannica.com/ebc/article-9070371

Science in India. (n.d.) In Indian Child Online. Retrieved 24 Nov 2006 from indianchild.com website: http://www.indianchild.com/indian_ scientists.htm

Subhas Chandra Bose. (n.d.) In All India Congress Committee website. Retrieved 6 Dec 2006 from http://www.aicc.org.in/subhas_chandra_ bose.php

Thapar. R (2002) *Sakuntala. Text, Readings, Histories*. London: Anthem Press

US Can't Take India For Granted. (23 Nov 2006). In The Straits Times, p. 29.

Waterstone, R. (1996). *India: Belief And Ritual, The Gods And The Cosmos, Meditation And The Yogic Arts*. London: Duncan Baird Publishers

Winternitz, M. (1996). *A History of Indian Literature, (Vol 1)*. Delhi: Motilal Banarsidass

ABOUT THE

A U T H O R

ANJANA MOTIHAR CHANDRA is a freelance journalist with extensive experience in writing and editing, having worked in news agencies as well as newspapers, magazines, public relations and publishing during her long career. She received her Master of Mass Communication from Nanyang Technological University (NTU) in Singapore and has taught academic writing and communication to undergraduate students there. Anjana is widely travelled and has lived in such diverse regions as North America, Africa and the Middle East. She has been living in Singapore with her husband and two children for the past seven years.

ACKNOWLEDGEMENTS

The author would like to thank M.R. Narayanswamy, Lee Mei Lin and Wee Wong for their kind help and support in writing this book. She would also like to acknowledge the valuable contribution made by Rajive, Ritika and Anantya Chandra, Ratan, Pushpa and Renuka Motihar and Surabhi Bikhchandani, without whom this book would not have been possible.

INDEX